*The*

# OFFICIAL KIDS' SURVIVAL

*Kit*

## Other Books by Pat Fortunato

WHEN WE WERE YOUNG: AN ALBUM OF STARS

ADVICE FROM THE SUPERSTARS

ROCK 'N' ROLL PUZZLES

FOOZLES

SPACED-OUT FOOZLES

DINO-MITE FOOZLES

ALL-AMERICAN FOOZLES

# The OFFICIAL KIDS' SURVIVAL Kit

## How to Do Things on Your Own

*Elaine Chaback and Pat Fortunato*

ILLUSTRATIONS BY BILL OGDEN

Little, Brown and Company · Boston · Toronto

C

LIBRARY OF CONGRESS CATALOGING IN PUBLICATION DATA

Chaback, Elaine.
    The official kids' survival kit.

    Summary: An alphabetical handbook giving practical advice to help in coping with
everyday situations and routines as well as in handling accidents and common medical
emergencies.
    1. Children—United States—Life skills guides—Juvenile literature. 2. Home econom-
ics—United States—Handbooks, manuals, etc.—Juvenile literature. [1. Life skills—
Handbooks, manuals, etc. 2. Home economics—Handbooks, manuals, etc. 3. First aid—
Handbooks, manuals, etc.]
I. Fortunato, Pat.  II. Title.
HQ781.C49    640'.88054    81-11743
ISBN 0-316-13531-3         AACR2

VB
Designed by Susan Windheim
*Published simultaneously in Canada*
*by Little, Brown & Company (Canada) Limited*

PRINTED IN THE UNITED STATES OF AMERICA

For our kids:
*Leah,*
who provided the inspiration, and
*Harry,*
who provided the Mallomars

# ACKNOWLEDGMENTS

This book was compiled with the help of many, but wc are especially grateful to Cheryl Gotthelf, our research editor, for her enthusiasm, energy, and total commitment to this book.

We are also indebted to Mark Saltzman, our editorial consultant, whose suggestions were invaluable.

And, finally, a very special *thank you* to our panel of experts: Lewis Brey (age 12), Leah Chaback (age 13), Keith Eiger (age 10), Doug McAdoo (age 14), Michael McBride (age 11), and Teresa Mizelle (age 12).

# ❧ FOREWORD ❧

## To the Parent

*The Official Kids' Survival Kit* is a reference source to help children become more self-sufficient. It is also for you: the working parent, the divorced or single parent, the busy parent, the concerned parent.

You can see by the table of contents that the book deals with a wide range of topics, from coping with everyday situations and routines to more serious concerns of some children — how to deal with loneliness, boredom, jealousy, and fears — to handling accidents and common medical emergencies.

*The Official Kids' Survival Kit* will be more personal — and therefore more helpful — if you will participate in its use by going through it carefully and making notes where necessary. At the end of the sections that deal mainly with emergencies and household chores, there is space for you to add special notes. This means *anything* that might apply specifically to your child and to your household: for example, under PET CARE, you may need to add *"Never* give Fido milk"; or even, in the section on EMERGENCIES, "I don't agree with this. Call me at work *anytime!!"* In this way, you can make this book your personal representative.

*The Official Kids' Survival Kit* — indeed, any book — cannot be a substitute for parental guidance; but we sincerely hope that it will provide your child, in the absence of an adult, with useful and necessary information.

# ❦ INTRODUCTION ❦

## To the Reader

*The Official Kids' Survival Kit* is here to help you handle little things with ease, and big things without panic. In a way, it's more than just survival: it's learning how to be on top of many things most of the time. But don't get the wrong idea: no one (repeat: *no one*) thinks that this book will turn you into a perfect person who can do everything.

What it will do is give you a place to turn to for information you need. It can make you aware of things you've never thought of before, and help you with things that have puzzled or frightened you in the past. That way, you can face your problems, tackle them, and have a fighting chance of coming out a winner.

You can read *The Official Kids' Survival Kit* from cover to cover, or by skipping around from topic to topic. Be sure to check the cross-references, though. When you come to the words "See also," you'll know that another section in the book has more information on the subject you're reading about. For instance, the section on JOBS — FOR YOU may help you if you want to know about BABYSITTING. And check out ALLOWANCE if you're interested in MONEY. It's also a good idea to read the FOREWORD, even though it's written for parents. After all, we are all in this together.

# ᔍᕗ CONTENTS ᔍᕗ

## D Through E

## Just F

## G Through H

## I Through K

## L Through M

*Just*

# ☞ ❧ ACCIDENT PREVENTION ❧

Someone once described a sloppy character he knew as "an accident looking for a place to happen." It's often true. Sure, some accidents can't be prevented, but many accidents don't happen entirely "by accident," they happen because people get careless. Nobody's perfect, and you can't do every little thing right, every single time. But you can be careful when it counts. Especially when you're alone, or when you're in charge of young children.

Accident prevention is mostly common sense. Anyone who goes around throwing banana peels on the floor, or running down the hall with a pair of long, sharp, pointed scissors, is headed for trouble. Be aware of what's going on around you, and watch out for dangerous situations. If you see that a fishbowl has been placed on top of the refrigerator, move it someplace safer before it moves itself — onto someone's head (maybe yours). You can't foresee every problem or prevent every accident, but you can use your head for better things than catching falling fishbowls.

## Common Sense in the Kitchen

Certain areas in the house are more accident-prone than others. One such spot is the kitchen, and the worst danger is fire. Keep matches out of the hands of babes (this goes for *anywhere* in the house). And be careful when you're using them yourself. Never toss a match into the garbage unless you're sure it's out. When you light a gas broiler with a match, be sure that the gas has only been on for a few seconds. The combination of too much gas escaping and a lighted match can cause quite a blast, and not the kind you'd like to get caught in. For safety's sake, lean as far back as you can when lighting it, with your hair (if it's long) tied back and out of the way. And don't light it at all if you haven't been shown how.

When you're working at the stove, keep pot handles facing inward, toward the back of the stove. That way, pots are less likely to be knocked over by flying elbows. And dress in something that makes sense.

You probably don't wear robes with long, flowing sleeves anyway. But in case you get the urge to, and you also want to do some serious cooking, choose one or the other — not both.

Don't leave anything made of paper or cloth — paper towels, bags, containers, napkins, pot holders — on the stove top (a good way to start a small fire), and never leave the house when anything is cooking (a good way to let a small fire get out of control). It's also best to keep young children away from the stove, and out of the kitchen altogether, if that's possible. (Sharp objects and cleaning materials, which can act as poisons, are often stored here.)

Another source of danger in the kitchen is sharp utensils, such as knives. Of course, you're careful when you're cutting something. But also be aware of where you've put down knives and other utensils when you're not using them. Knife holders are best, where you can't accidentally cut yourself, and if you have a silverware holder on your dish drainer, put knives and forks in upside down, so you won't get poked. There's also the danger of leaving a can hanging around after you've opened it. Those edges are rough, and can give nasty cuts. Get into the habit of cleaning as you go, and you'll not only have less mess, you'll have less danger.

## Bathroom Baddies

The baddies of the bathroom world (accidentally speaking) are razors, scissors, and . . . soap. Right, soap. Sure, razors and scissors can cut, but soap, left on the floor or in the bathtub, can make you slip — a very common household accident. Put sharp or slippery things away even if someone else has left them around, and clean up after yourself. And remember, rubber duckies cause accidents, too.

## Watch That Medicine Cabinet

Medicines can also be a problem. Don't let any child near the medicine cabinet. Young children will put almost anything into their mouths. If you have to give them medicine, never call it "candy" — they might think all those pretty pills are candy, too. And before you take anything yourself, be sure to check the label. Many pills look alike, and it's easy to make a mistake.

## Allover Safety

You can also avoid many accidents by following these tips:

- *Treat all electrical appliances with great respect.* Read the section on APPLIANCES, and if you have a question about a particular appliance, check to see if there is a special section for that. If anything — a cord, plug, socket — looks suspicious, tell a parent about it right away
- *Don't litter.* Pick up your belongings — clothes, games, equipment — rather than leaving them around where someone (even you) could trip over them.
- *Take it easy.* Don't play roughhouse games where things can easily be broken: the kitchen, bathroom, or anywhere where there's glass, china, or lamps.

## ACCIDENTS

An accident can be anything from a broken glass to a broken bone. No matter what happens, *don't panic!* Think. Then do whatever you can yourself, and get help — quickly — if you need it.

See also ACCIDENT PREVENTION, FIRST AID, and BROKEN DISHES/GLASS.

# ACNE

What do you call it when you get five bright red pimples in a row? A royal flush? A royal pain in the neck? Nope, you call it acne. (In "Acne Poker," a game we invented to keep ourselves laughing about our blemishes — so we wouldn't cry — three pimples and two blackheads, or vice versa, are a full house, which definitely beat out four of a kind: pimples, blackheads, or whiteheads.)

You say you have acne and you don't see anything funny about it? Well, maybe you're right. But it is *not* the end of the world. If it were, we'd be in big trouble, because about 80 percent of teenagers and many adults have it to some degree.

Why? No one knows for sure, and that's unfortunate. If there were a definite cause, there would probably be a surefire cure by now. But there isn't. Sure, experts agree that excess oil in the skin — which is produced like mad during adolescence — has something to do with it. But exactly how it happens is not yet known. And there is a lot of disagreement about whether eating certain foods, especially chocolate and fried foods, causes acne or makes it worse.

However, there has been a lot of study on the subject, and enough is known about acne for you to launch a good, strong attack against it. Here's a four-step plan that's helped many people, doesn't cost a lot of money, and is definitely worth trying.

## STEP ONE: CLEAN WITH CARE

This is probably the most important thing you need to know about skin care. Who says? Many dermatologists (skin doctors) and cosmetologists (skin-care specialists). Keeping it clean is essential to keeping it clear. The only problem is that plain old soap and water may not be enough when you have acne. In fact, some soaps contain fats or creams, which are not good for you at all. And harsh soaps or really rough scrubbings can irritate the skin and make the whole thing worse. So, you have to find a mild soap that works for you, and — here's the important part — be consistent. Clean regularly (at least twice a day), and be gentle. Use warm (not hot) water and rinse with cool (not cold) water.

You can choose a particular brand of cleanser or acne lotion on the advice of a druggist, your parents, or a friend who has the same problem and is solving it. Many cleansers are good, but you have to try them out to see how your skin reacts to them. If your face gets very dry, flaky, patchy, or just breaks out even more, then change cleansers — fast.

## STEP TWO: HANDS OFF

You've been told this before, many more times than you'd care to remember, but don't keep touching your face, leaning your chin on your hands, or (worst of all) picking at your pimples. (Yecch.) You've probably been told that the reason for this hands-off policy is that you spread germs (bacteria, really) on your skin. This is true enough, but the more important reason is that you're putting too much pressure on your pores, which are enlarged already, and that makes the situation worse.

## STEP THREE: DON'T ADD OIL TO OIL

If you've got acne, you've got too much oil in your skin. So it doesn't make any sense to add more with heavy creams and lotions. If your skin becomes dry from over-cleaning, it will usually correct itself in a few days. But if you must use a moisturizer, make sure it's not oily or thick.

As we've said, doctors disagree on exactly what effect diet has on your complexion. But it is a good idea to cut down on oils, fatty foods, sweets, and colas, if you tend to eat too much of these things. (See the section on NUTRITION.) Eating well will help you stay healthy, and good health is important for good skin.

## STEP FOUR: CLEANER THAN CLEAN

Even if you "Clean with Care," keep your "Hands Off," and "Don't Add Oil to Oil," your skin still might not be clean enough if you've got acne. There's more! Get into the habit of giving your skin a deep-cleaning treatment once or twice a week. You can try special products, such as acne scrub pads, cleansing grains, or exfoliating (peeling) lotions. Follow the directions, and don't get carried away. If it says to use the product every other day, don't fool yourself into thinking that if you use it *every* day, your skin will get better twice as fast. It doesn't work that way. You'll probably just dry up your face, and end up with peeling skin — *and* acne.

## The Squeeze

Should you *ever* squeeze pimples? NO. That's the way to get scars. What about blackheads? Sometimes. But only if you learn to do it properly: squeezing gently with your fingertips, not your nails, with your hands super clean, and using alcohol before and afterward. Your face should also be very clean and warmed up with hot towels to open the pores. *Never* force a blackhead. If it doesn't come out easily, leave it alone and try again in a few days. And never squeeze a blackhead if there's any redness around it.

## (If All Else Fails) Wear a Mask

This is not the kind of mask you use on Halloween. It's something you smear on your face, and which gets hard and makes you look like "The Beast That Borrowed Brooklyn." But when you rinse it off, your skin looks better, because the mask has a vacuum-cleaner effect, drawing out the stuff that was stuck in your pores.

Masks — also called masques — come in many disgusting colors, from gruesome gray to putrid puce. (Some masks are called *mud packs,* for a very good reason.)

The idea is not to look nice while it's on, but to help your face look better after it's off. That's why so many women (and recently, men) spend a lot of money at health spas and salons to "wear" these ridiculous-looking masks for fifteen minutes or more. Some people go regularly, because the effect builds up: the more you use them, the better your skin gets. Some masks even peel off in one piece, which is kind of fun, if you like that sort of thing.

And even if they don't clear up your complexion (although they probably will help) you can have a lot of fun running around with a green face, scaring the pants off your little brother. By the way, a great mask you can make yourself is plain yogurt (hold the berries). Use it sparingly and rinse it off when it's dry.

## Sun

Getting a tan makes your skin look better, but don't get burned. This only damages the skin even more.

## Relax

*Relax!??!!?!* First you have all these zits, see, then you read this book that tells you four thousand things to do about them, and then you're supposed to relax! Sure. Well, try. Many doctors feel that being tense makes acne worse. It may even be the reason that adults — well past adolescence — have breakouts from time to time. Don't worry so much about your skin, do something about it. (*Please* read the section on WORRYING.) And if you're under a lot of pressure, learn to relax more often.

## "But I've Tried Everything!!"

If you really have tried to clear up your skin (*really trying* means doing something constructive about it for at least two months) and it hasn't improved, or if you have very severe acne, then you should see a dermatologist. It's best to try to deal with it on your own first, but if it's really bothering you, then don't hesitate. Talk it over with your folks, and when you see a doctor, follow his or her instructions to the letter!

## ❧ AIR CONDITIONERS ❧

### Be Cool

Okay, it's hot, hot, hot, and you have permission to turn on the air conditioner. All you have to do is push a button or turn a knob, so what's the problem?

No problem. But there are two things you should know to be cool about air conditioning:

1. Be sure to close all the windows and doors in the room. If you don't, the cool air will go right out the window.

2. If you turn the air conditioner off and

then want to start it again, wait about five minutes before you turn it on. The motor needs the rest, and quick restarts can blow a fuse. Then everyone will be hot under the collar.

See also APPLIANCES.

♦ NOTES:

## ◈ ALLOWANCE ◈

### Who's Afraid of the Big, Bad Budget?

The person who invented The Allowance must have been a wise and wonderful soul. Now, if only someone could invent a way to make the money last from one allowance to the next. Well, in a way, it's been done. It's called The Budget. Wait! Stop! Don't run away in horror and fear. The word *budget* isn't as bad as it sounds.

The bad part is that you can never get every single thing you want, or do every single thing you want to do. (Even if you had the money, you'd run out of time.) So you have to decide on your *priorities*, which is a fancy way of saying that you have to figure out what's important and what's not. The good part is that when you do sit down and plan it out, you usually end up getting more than you would have if you followed your whims and blew the money on the first thing that caught your eye.

To plan a budget, you first have to figure out how much money you have coming in. Is it just allowance? Or do you have a job, too? Total it up and write it down.

Then consider how the money goes (we will *not* accept "very quickly" as an answer). What is your allowance supposed to cover? In some families, it's for some school expenses, such as carfare and lunches, and the rest is *discretionary income* (which is a fancy term for "you can do

$ $ $ $

anything you want with it"). In other families, your whole allowance is yours to do with as you like, and you get extra money for life's little necessities.

Make a list of what you spend your money on, and approximately how much each thing costs. You don't have to be a

$3.00 - $3.73 = problems

mathematical genius to know that if you've got three dollars coming in and three seventy-three going out, you're in trouble. Something's got to go. And that's when you make the decisions. The movie or the book? The book or the poster? The poster or the popcorn? Listen to your head, your heart, and your stomach. You'll make the right choices.

## Making Allowance(s)

Every kid doesn't get the same allowance any more than every adult gets the same salary. You are faced with the same problem your parents have: how to do the most with what you've got. Of course, if you really think you need more, you should talk it over with your folks. It's like asking for a raise. They could say "no way," but they might say "okay," if you present them with a good case. Tell them what your expenses are and why you're having a hard time. No one has to remind them about inflation, but adults sometimes do forget that a candy bar doesn't cost a nickel anymore.

On the other hand, *you* have to make allowances when your parents are having hard times with money. There may be times when there simply isn't enough money to allow an allowance. Don't make your parents feel any worse than they do by nagging them about it. If you really need more money, or if you don't get an allowance at all, see the section JOBS — FOR YOU.

## And Now a Word about Saving

Can you take it? Well, you've survived reading about budgets, haven't you? (Or have you?) Saving sounds like such a safe, dull, boring, unexciting thing to do. You've got that money and you want to spend it — *all* of it — *now*. But if you can manage to save a little, a little at a time, after a while you'll have a bigger amount than you ever had at one time, and you can use it to get something you really want. And that's not hard to take at all.

See also MONEY.

# Anger

See ARGUMENTS.

# Animal Bites

See BITES.

# Animals

See PET CARE.

## ❧ APPEARANCE ❧

### Here's Looking at You, Kid!

The key to good looks is good health: eating the right foods, getting enough sleep and exercise, and just plain taking care of yourself.

After that comes grooming: making sure that you (and your clothes) are neat and clean. Good grooming is the surest, easiest way to make the best of what you've got, because it's something you have real control over. With a little soap, shampoo, and good sense, you can come out looking great. Or, you can forget about grooming altogether, and end up looking like a movie star: The Creature from the Black Lagoon!

### Hair Today . . .

Nobody is saying that you have to be perfect. Everybody looks scruffy some of the time — especially when working or playing hard. But some things are a real turn-off. Like stringy, greasy hair. And the thing is, it's really not that hard to make it full and shiny.

You can use whatever shampoo your

that's when to stop washing it and give it a *good* rinse. Rinse your hair really well, making sure that every trace of shampoo is gone, because suds left in the hair make it dull and can attract dirt.

## Let's Face It

Besides your hair, the first thing that most people notice about you is your face. You may never, in your whole life, win a beauty contest, but your face can be clean. And so can your hands and nails. (Just wash up at least twice a day.) It's not that hard to do. And nobody will believe your story about wanting to conserve water!

## The Whole Tooth

You say you've run out of toothpaste and you can't brush your pearly whites? Well, they won't be pearly white very long if you don't brush them. Anyway, you don't

family buys, but if you have a choice, ask which one is the mildest and pick that one. How often you shampoo depends on your hair, but if you find that you have to wash it every day — and many people do — then give it only one sudsing, not two as the directions on most shampoo bottles suggest. After a while, you'll get to know when your hair is squeaky clean, and

need toothpaste. (Sorry about that.) In a real pinch, just use a brush and water. The important thing is to remove the pieces of food that give you cavities, not to mention bad breath.

Rinsing your mouth after eating will also help to keep your teeth clean, as will using dental floss.

Don't believe the commercials that tell you that your whole life will change if your teeth sparkle and your breath is fresh

(we *told* you not to mention bad breath!). But if you brush regularly you will have a nice smile, and that's not bad.

## Fuddy Duddies

Some people think it's old fashioned to have clean, unwrinkled clothes. Maybe. How do the people you admire look most of the time? Like they just had a fight with a large, unclean warthog — and lost? Like they had slept in their clothes — for the entire month of November? Like they had inherited a lifetime supply of bear grease — and wanted to use it up in a single day? We doubt it. Most likely their duds are reasonably fresh and clean, with buttons buttoned, zippers zipped and shoelaces laced.

You get to look that way by hanging up or folding your clean clothes (see CLOTH-ING CARE and LAUNDRY), and by taking a minute to check yourself out after you've dressed. This is a minute well spent. People will be looking at you all day. Why not be "looking good"?

See also ACNE, DIETING, and EXERCISE, if they apply to you.

# APPLIANCES

## Know before You Go

Before you go ahead and use the washing machine, dishwasher, air conditioner — *any* electrical appliance — be sure you know how it works. There's a very good

reason for this: you could get hurt! Not only that: you could break something, and that means that your parent may have to pay for expensive repairs or go out and buy a new appliance. This is guaranteed *not* to make you the most popular person in your household.

## Take an Appliance Tour

If we tried to give you step-by-step instructions for every make and model of every appliance ever made, this would turn into a 150,000-page book (and we'd probably overlook *your* brand of dish-

washer, anyway). The best thing you can do is to ask how each appliance works. Let your parent take you on a tour of your home to show you how to work every appliance you are allowed to use. Find out how to work all the buttons and knobs and switches and dials. Find out if an appliance has to be unplugged after its use. Ask if specific electrical outlets have to be used for certain appliances. And if any appliance in your home has a quirk, find out what it is. (You may have to give the washing machine a gentle rap before the rinse cycle, or set the toaster to "dark" if you want your toast "light," or the air conditioner to "warmer" when you want it "cooler.") If there is anything that isn't absolutely clear, *ask questions!*

If your family uses a neighborhood coin-operated washing machine, dryer, and/or dry-cleaning machine, find out how these work, too.

## Check It Out

When using any appliance, check out certain things, and if anything's wrong, tell your parents about it.

• Look at the cord and plug. If the cord is frayed or ripped, or if the plug is cracked, loose, or in any way damaged, do not use the appliance. It could be a fire hazard.

• Don't overload electrical outlets by using too many appliances at once. This can blow a fuse and cut off your electricity. Check with a parent to find out what is safe for your home.

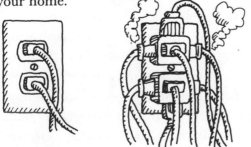

• If an appliance is on fire, follow the steps in the section on FIRE. (It would be a good idea to read that section *now*, since it might be too late once a fire has started.)

• Never, never, *never* plug or unplug an appliance — or handle anything else electrical — with wet hands. You'll be in for a shock!

• If you do get a minor electrical shock from an appliance (with dry hands), or if you see any sparks or smoke, disconnect the appliance right away and do not use it.

• If an appliance doesn't work, first check to see that it's connected. If it's plugged in and it still doesn't work, it could mean that it needs a repair or that a fuse is blown (see page 94 for replacing a fuse).

• Never grab the cord and yank the plug out of the wall outlet. Hold the plug between your fingers and remove it gently from the outlet.

• If you suddenly feel like cleaning an appliance, follow the manufacturer's or your parent's instructions. Never clean an appliance while it's plugged in or turned on. And never put a small appliance (such as a toaster or blender) into water unless the instructions say it's safe.

• If your parent has asked you not to use a certain appliance, don't use it — even if it's listed in this book. Your parent has an excellent reason for giving you those instructions.

## Look It Up

As we said before, step-by-step instructions for every appliance are not given in this book. But we have included tips on using some of the appliances you're most likely to find in your home: AIR CONDITIONERS, BLENDERS/FOOD PROCESSORS, DISHWASHERS, irons (IRONING), washing machines and dryers (LAUNDRY: *By Machine*), TOASTERS, MICROWAVE OVENS, STEREOS, and VACUUM CLEANERS.

◆ NOTES:

_____
_____
_____
_____
_____

## ✌ APPOINTMENTS ✌

### Late Is Not Great

Some people think it's cool to be late. (But then, some people think it's cool to wear electric bow ties.) The truth is, whenever you make someone wait, you make someone angry. If you're late once, they may not say anything about it. But if you're late all the time, the anger builds up.

Whenever you have an appointment — with a team, a tutor, your piano teacher, the people you're babysitting for, your parents, your friends, a doctor or dentist — always try to be on time. Sure, once in a while you'll be late. Things

happen that you just can't help. But when that's the case, try to call and let the person know. And never, never just let someone go on waiting when you're not going to come. That's the pits!

### Forget It?

If you have the habit of forgetting appointments, try one of these ideas:

• Write yourself little notes and leave them in places you can't miss: with your bus fare or house keys, in a schoolbook you'll be using, in your baseball glove, on top of the cookie jar . . .

• Ask a parent to leave you a note that you'll be sure to see the minute you get home from school. Or ask a friend you can count on to remind you about your date.

### And Don't Forget Your Parents

• If all else fails, pin a note to your shirt. You can write the note backwards, so you will read it every time you look in a mirror! (This is for extreme situations only.)

If you've made an appointment but forgot to tell your parents about it, leave them a note or call them to explain where you are and when you'll be home.

## ❧ ARGUMENTS ❧

### Fighting with Friends

*True* ☐ or *False* ☐ : You should never have an argument with a good friend. *False!* No two people agree all the time, so if you

never argue with someone, you're probably not being honest. Many people believe that a good argument clears the air, and that seems to be *True*. You have your say, others have their say, and everything is out in the open.

## Once You Say It, It's Said

The big danger with arguing is that you'll say something you'll regret. Sure, you can apologize later. But saying that you didn't really mean it doesn't quite make up for your having said it in the first place. The first rule of arguing is:

1. Talk about the specific thing that's bothering you — don't call names. It's one thing to tell someone that you're angry because they didn't share their game with you. It's another thing to call that person a "mean, stupid, selfish creep."

There are rules for arguing? Why not? There are rules for professional fighters, aren't there? And if you don't know how to deal with an argument, it can turn into a nasty fight and/or the end of a beautiful friendship. Some other rules are:

2. Don't wait until you're boiling mad before you talk about what's bothering you. If you ignore your anger for a long time, it could finally explode over some silly thing. You might even end up feeling foolish for losing your cool when you really do have a good reason to gripe.

*Example:* Every day, at least once, your friend forgets something — his pencil, his books, his lunch money, his head! And every day you lend him the thing he's missing. For weeks, you say nothing. Then one day, he asks you for your last sheet of paper, and you flip out. If anyone saw you blowing your top over one piece of looseleaf, they'd think you were nuts. And you are — for letting it reach the point where it really gets to you. Somewhere along the line, you should have sat your friend down and said, "Hey, look, I really like you a lot and I think you're nice and all that, *but . . .* all this borrowing is beginning to bug me."

3. If you lose control, or if another person blows up at you in anger, try to wait until everyone calms down before you talk about the problem. It's very hard to reason when you're angry. That's why people count to ten before they speak.

4. Tell your side of the story, but listen to the other person's point of view, too. Even if you're right, you're probably not 100 percent right.

5. Don't think you've always got to "win." If you're wrong, admit it. Say you're sorry and get on with the friendship. And sometimes, you just have to "agree to disagree."

6. Try to learn something from these arguments. If you did something wrong, think about how you could correct it in the future. Even if you think you were right, consider if you were too tough (or too easy) on your friend.

## Family Feuds

The rules above hold true for fights with brothers and sisters, too. It's even more important to understand arguments with them because you live with them. For more about the causes and cures, read the section on BROTHERS AND SISTERS.

The rules also apply for arguments with your folks, except for one thing: they usually win. When all else fails, parents like to remind you that, after all, they *are* your parents and you should listen to them. *Sigh.* Face it, they're often right. And even when they're wrong, their motives are usually good.

One more thing: when you fight with your family, you can't just go home and forget it. That's why no one really wins or loses. And unlike the families you see on TV, real families rarely have fights with neat, simple solutions that leave everybody happy. Before you start a yelling match that ends in tears and bad feelings, count to ten, maybe a hundred and ten, count your blessings, and, if you have to argue, follow the rules.

## When Parents Fight

It can be frightening. Even if it's just a small disagreement, you may feel very uncomfortable. The first thing many kids think is that, somehow, it's all their fault.

It isn't. Even if your parents are arguing about you, they alone are responsible for their actions. Many times you have absolutely nothing to do with it: they may even be using you as an excuse to fight because they're angry about something else. And that's certainly not your fault. Remember that even if you weren't in the picture, they would still have arguments.

Some kids worry that anytime their parents fight it means that they don't love each other anymore, and may even get divorced. Of course, a steady diet of fighting can lead to separation. But even the happiest couple disagree from time to time. And there will always be family arguments.

No one expects you to enjoy your parents' arguments (or anyone else's, for that matter). But if the arguments aren't too severe or too frequent, you can learn not to get too upset about them.

*Just*

# Babies

See BABYSITTING and INFANTS.

# ᪥ BABYSITTING ᪥

All babysitting jobs are not created equal. Some are really "sitting" situations, and practically no more than that. The children may be asleep when you arrive, and your job is simply to be there until the parents come back home. But sometimes there's lots more: making meals, getting the kids to bed, playing games, reading stories. So with every babysitting job, you've got to find out exactly what you're supposed to do.

## Questions and Answers

Maybe the parent will tell you everything you need to know. But don't count on it. Before you're left alone with kids, make sure you have answers to questions like these:

- Do you have to prepare a meal or snack?

- If so, what should you feed them and where are all the things you'll need?

- Is there anything special you should know about any of the children, such as medication to be taken while you're there?

- What time do the kids have to go to bed?

- Should you leave a night-light on?

- When will the parents be home?

- Where can they — or someone they trust — be reached, just in case?

## Safety First

It's also a good idea to have a list of emergency numbers — police, fire department, family doctor — near the phone. Remember, the most important part of your job is keeping the children from being harmed. You can do this by following the general suggestions under ACCIDENT PREVENTION and SAFETY AND SECURITY, and by using your own good sense (such as not telling a stranger on the phone that you're baby-sitting). If anything does happen, get help — fast!

## Getting Down to Business

Tell the parents what your rates are before you do your job. If your rates go up after a certain time, make this clear.

## You're in Charge

The parents leave and (*gulp*) it's all up to you. How you behave now is very important. Be firm, but don't act like a Marine drill sergeant in a bad movie. Don't make a big deal out of small things, and don't make idle threats ("You'd better . . . or else!"). But don't let the children get away with things you know their parents wouldn't like ("You say you *always* dance in the rain in a bathing suit?" No way!).

Since you are in charge, and since you're older (and bigger) than they are, the children will usually listen to you. Usually. If they don't, try giving them a stern look, or raising your voice — a *little,* and not very often. But if this doesn't work, and you come to the conclusion that you have major brats on your hands, do the best you can and talk it over with the parents when they come home. If you've been fair, and you tell the story honestly,

you don't have to feel that you're being a rat by telling on the kids.

A good way to get young children to behave is to make them feel important by asking them to help you. Try to get the older ones to help the younger ones, without letting the big kids boss the little ones around. In general, treat the kids in your care the way you'd like your parents to treat you.

## Doing Their Thing

Play games that are not too rowdy — build models, work a jigsaw puzzle, color, or draw. Help them with their homework if they ask, but don't do it for them. And let them choose the TV show — unless it's something you know (and they know) is a no-no.

Some babysitters make up a kit and carry it with them in a small suitcase or tote bag. The kit might contain:

crayons and pencils  
blunt scissors  
colored paper  
small, safe toys  

balls and balloons  
storybooks  
magazines  
playing cards  

## Bedtime

You know how they feel. They want to stay up "just a little longer." Sorry, no deal. Stick to the time the parents requested, and be very pleasant but very insistent. You can make the whole thing a lot more fun by reading a story *after* the child is in bed — the promise of being read to will probably make washing up and changing into pajamas go a little faster, too. Whatever you do, don't play roughhouse games just before bedtime, and don't just order the kids to go to their rooms alone. (For how to handle it if a child is frightened, read *Children's Fears* on page 114.)

When they're finally asleep, check on them about every half hour to make sure everything is okay. If they wake up and want a drink of water, bring it to them — once, or twice at the most. After that, tell them that water service is off for the night, and wish them "pleasant dreams."

## Behave — Yourself

Okay, you've got the kids behaving and everything is under control. What about your own behavior? Remember, you're getting paid to do a job; not to talk on the phone for hours or to eat everything in the refrigerator (and the freezer, and the cupboard, and the cookie jar, and . . . ). Never invite a friend over unless you've cleared it ahead of time with the parents. And use your head on this one. Another person to study with may be fine, but a pajama party is out!

Also check out ENTERTAINING CHILDREN, FEARS, FIRST AID, INFANTS, and SEXUAL ADVANCES.

# ❧ BED-MAKING ❧

## Start at the Bottom

Most bottom sheets are fitted, so they're no problem to put on. Just make sure you've got the corners of the sheet on the corners of the bed, evenly all around, so that the corners won't pull out after one night's sleep.

If you use flat sheets for the bottom, follow our directions for top sheets and blankets, but leave enough sheet at the top to tuck it in.

## Then Get on Top of It

*Step One:* Place the sheet over the bed, lining up the top of the sheet with the top of the mattress, letting the extra material fall over at the foot end.

*Step Two:* Tuck in the sides (flap A).

*Step Three:* Lift flap B out and over the bed. It will make a kind of triangle.

*Step Four:* Tuck the bottom part of flap B in.

*Step Five:* Then let the top of flap B hang down.

*Step Six:* Tuck in flap B.

To do the other half, just follow the same steps on the other side.

## Covering Up

If there's a bedspread or quilt, put it on neatly, with about the same amount of material hanging over each side.

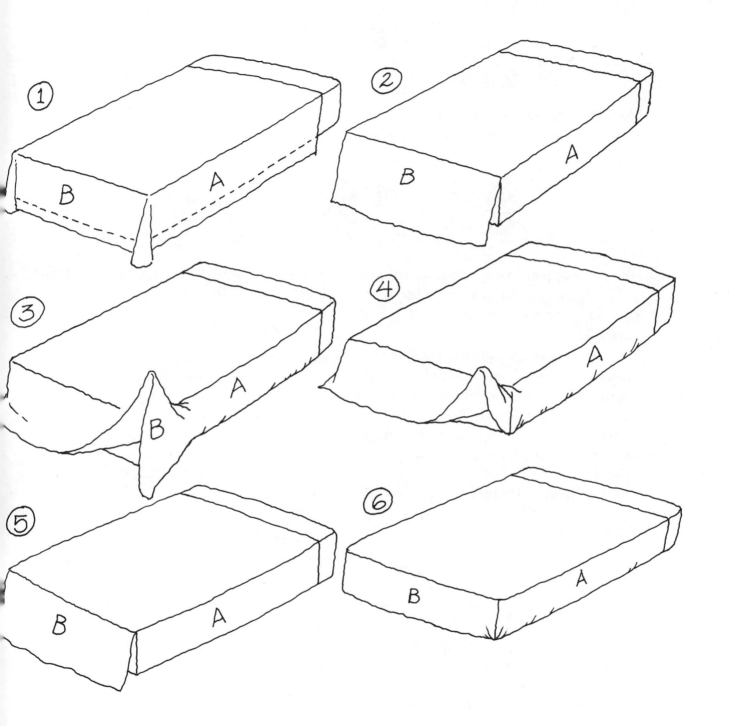

# ☙ BEE STINGS ❧

## Ouch!

Most bee stings are just a pain in the neck — or the finger, or the foot, or wher-

ever you happen to get stung. But if you get stung, call your doctor right away. You're probably not in real danger, just in pain.

☛ However, some people can become very sensitive or severely allergic to bee stings, so getting stung can be very serious. If you see that the person is having trouble breathing or swallowing, is vomiting, weak, nauseated, or even unconscious, get a doctor — *fast!*

If the stinger is stuck in the wound, scrape it away with a butter knife or tongue depressor, or pull it out with tweezers. Then wash gently with soap and water. You can use an ice pack to help relieve the swelling.

See also FIRST AID.

◆ NOTES:

_____
_____
_____
_____
_____

# ☙ BICYCLES ❧

## The Bike of Your Dreams

Bikes come in all sorts of shapes and sizes, and it's easy to get carried away (rolled away?) by the fanciest, flashiest model. But before you ask for that fifteen-speed extravaganza, think about what you'll be using your bike for. Will it be just for fun, for a paper route or deliveries, riding to school, or racing on a team? The answer you give should help you and your folks make the right choice.

Your three basic bikes are:

*Middleweight:* Good for beginners because it's easy to balance at slow speeds.

*High-rise:* It can turn on a dime, but takes more skill to ride.

*Lightweight:* Strong and fast — the best bike for long rides and races.

## SPEED DEMONS

Now, what about speeds? Should you get a three-speed bike, a ten-speed, or what? The ordinary no-frills bike — one with no gears at all — is fine for many people. Just because it has no gears, and no "speed" in its name, doesn't mean that you can't go fast. You'll just have to pedal harder at higher speeds. The benefit of a three-speed is that you can go faster without working so much. But there is a catch: you have to learn to shift gears properly, or the bike won't work well. You can even damage your bike (badly) if you shift gears incor-

rectly. Ten-speed bikes are more complicated to operate, and are especially good for racing or cross-country riding.

## WHAT ABOUT SIZE?

Bikes are not like sweaters: you shouldn't buy one you'll "grow into." If you do, the bike will be too big right now, and that's not safe. You should be able to put one foot flat on the ground while the bike is perfectly upright. The other foot should reach the pedal without any trouble, with the knee slightly bent.

## The Safe Bike

Once you've got your best bike, make sure it's a safe bike, too. For starters, it should have front and rear reflectors, a bell or horn, and good brakes. Keep it in good shape with maintenance and repairs (there's more about that later in this section).

## Rolling Right Along

Bike riding is a skill, similar to driving a car, and you should be able to control your bike really well. When you were just learning, you practiced riding in a straight line, turning, stopping, starting up again, and looking over your left shoulder the way you'd have to do in traffic. It's not a bad idea to test these things again when

you're trying out a new bike, or if you haven't ridden for a long time.

## The Rules of the Road

You don't have to pass a driver's test, but you should know the traffic rules:

⊛ Always stay to the right, moving in the same direction as car traffic.

⊛ Obey *all* traffic regulations — stop signs, traffic lights, yield signals, and other markings.

⊛ Keep a safe distance between you and the vehicle in front of you.

⊛ Use hand signals when you're turning or stopping. (If you don't know them, ask your parents or contact your local motor vehicles bureau.)

⊛ Make your turns from the correct lane. This means that on a one-way street, you should be on the left for a left-hand turn, and on the right for a right-hand turn. On a

two-way street, stay as far to the left as possible for a left turn, and all the way to the right for a right turn. The idea is to go *with* the traffic, not to cut across it. If you have a tricky turn to make, stop on the corner and walk your bike across the street.

## The Best Biker

The best drivers don't just follow traffic rules. They also practice safety tips like these, which go for bike riders, too:

⊛ Drive your bike *defensively*. Watch out for the other guy, who might not be as good a rider (or driver) as you are.

⊛ Be extremely careful at all intersections, especially when making turns. (To be extra careful, walk your bike across intersections with the traffic light, if there is one.)

⊛ Watch out for hazards, such as drain grates, potholes, loose or bumpy gravel, hidden driveways, car doors opening.

⊛ Watch out for walkers (also known as pedestrians).

⊛ Ride single file with a group of friends on bikes.

⊛ Don't ride double — it interferes with your vision and your control.

⊛ *Never* "hitch" a ride by grabbing onto the back of a truck, bus, or anything else. Unexpected stops could mean disaster — for you.

⊛ Don't ride at night unless you have to. If you do, make sure your bike has rear reflectors and a headlight, and use clothing reflectors, too, if you have them. The point is *to be seen*.

⊛ Avoid riding in rainy or snowy weather, too, since slippery roads make stopping hard and skidding easy. If you must go out in bad weather, or if you get caught in rain or snow, *take it easy*.

⊛ Try to avoid crowded city streets — it's easy to run into people, especially children and elderly people.

⊛ In the country, stick to smaller roads whenever you can. Never ride your bike across a busy highway, but if you must ride on it, follow the rules of the road with *great caution*.

## Stop a Thief

Bike theft happens all the time. Instead of worrying about it, take these precautions:

⊛ Get a lock and chain, so you won't have to leave your bike hanging around ready for the taking. Chain it to something permanent — a bike rack, a tree, a tall metal pole or post. And make sure the chain is long enough to be pulled through a wheel and around the bike frame. Lock the chain.

⊛ Never leave your bike outside overnight in a place where it's likely to be stolen — even if it's chained up.

⊛ It's also a good idea to mark your bike with your name. You can even register it with the police, the way cars are registered, so that it can be identified in case of theft.

## Do-It-Yourself Bike Care

The better shape your bike is in, the less chance it'll break down and need a major overhaul by a professional. You can care for your bike yourself, part by part, like this:

⊛ *Chains:* They need to be cleaned and oiled from time to time, but this isn't difficult. You'll need a couple of clean rags, an old toothbrush, bicycle oil, and degreaser (or kerosene). Spray the rag with the degreaser and wipe the chain clean. Then scrub it with a toothbrush. Now put a bit of oil on the rollers and wipe it evenly over the chain with the other rag. We said a "bit" of oil because a little goes a long way. Too much will attract the dirt you're trying to get rid of in the first place.

⊛ *Brakes:* Keep them from squeaking or even breaking (get it? brakes? breaking?) by putting a little oil near the bolts.

⊛ *Tires:* They lose air as you ride, so keep them inflated. Follow the instructions from the manufacturer about the pressure.

⊛ *Frame:* A damp cloth and a bit of car wax can make your bike look clean and shiny, a regular mean machine.

## Flat Out!

Flat tires have a way of popping up (or in) at the worst times. But if you can learn to change the tires on your own bike, at least it won't be a major disaster.

1. The first step, and the hardest to explain, is taking the wheel off the bike. It's hard to explain because there is no standard way to remove a wheel from a bike — it depends on the type of bike you have. You'll have to find out how to do it for your bike by either reading the instructions or checking with your parents, service-station attendants, or bike-store people. It's not that hard to do, though, and once it's off, here's how to continue. . . .

2. Put the wheel on the floor and push down on the tire to get any air out of it.

3. With the wheel flat on the floor, peel one side of the tire off the rim, using your hands, a tire iron, or a spoon handle. Never use anything sharp, such as a knife or screwdriver, which could puncture the tube.

4. Slip the tube out of the tire, freeing the air valve first. Wash off the tube. Then fill it with air. Listen and feel around for the leak. If you can't find it, get a bucket or basin, fill it with water, and put the tube in it. Turn the tube and watch for bubbles, which will form where air is escaping. If there are bubbles coming from many parts of the tube, you may need a new one.

5. Unless the tube is hopeless, use a patch from a kit to repair it. You can get a patch

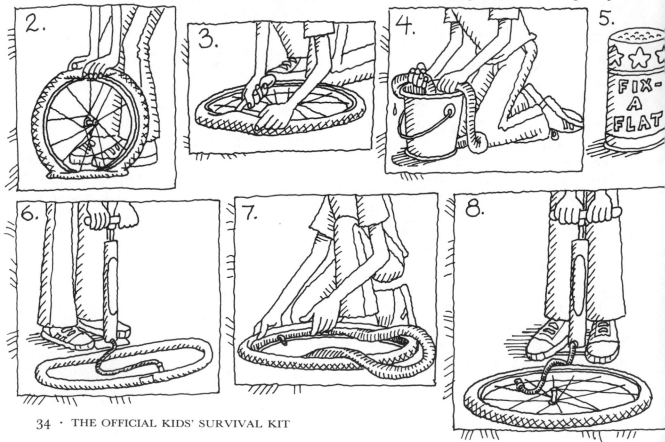

kit from most bicycle stores, and instructions are included.

6. Once the patch is in place and has dried, inflate the tube only enough to give it shape and get all the wrinkles out.

7. Slip the tube back into the tire, getting the air valve in place first.

8. Tuck the edge of the tire back into the rim, and fill the tire. As you're pumping the air into it, keep an eye on it to make sure the tire stays in place on the rim.

9. Put the wheel back on the bike. (Again,

all bikes are not the same, so you have to follow the instructions for your particular model, and/or get some help.)

## Other Repairs

Brakes and gears need to be fixed by parents or professionals. But if you stick to your side of the bargain — keeping the bike in good shape — you won't have so many repairs in the first place.

  BITES

## Animal Bites

Chances are, if you ever get bitten by an animal, it will be a small bite. You treat this as if it were an ordinary cut — by washing it out with soap and water and covering it with a bandage.

Always call a doctor even for a small bite, and get to the doctor right away if the bite is bad, if it's on the face, head, or neck, or if there's any chance that the animal has rabies. In any event, you may need a tetanus booster.

By the way, the size and seriousness of the bite is not the same thing as the size and seriousness of the animal. A small, innocent-looking rodent can sometimes do more damage than a big, frightening-looking dog.

*What is rabies?* Rabies is a very rare disease animals have that is very dangerous to humans. If you're bitten by an animal with rabies, and you don't get treatment, you'll die. Dogs in the United States don't carry rabies as often as raccoons, bats, foxes, or rats. But only a doctor can tell for sure. *You* can't. No, the dog doesn't have to be foaming at the mouth to have rabies. In fact, an animal can look healthy and still be diseased. That's why it's important to get the animal checked out. And that means remembering what it looked like and where it was, and reporting this to the police, your doctor, or a vet.

The treatment for preventing rabies is no fun. It hurts, and it makes some people feel very sick. But it's definitely much better than not getting it if you're in danger.

## Human Bites

Your little brother may snap at your fingers when you're trying to feed him. But it's really unusual to get a deep human bite. If the skin is broken, it can be dangerous, so wash the wound out very carefully with soap and water, and see a doctor right away. Sometimes you may need an antibiotic and/or a tetanus booster.

See also FIRST AID and BEE STINGS.

▶ NOTES:

_____
_____
_____
_____

   &#10670; BLACKOUTS &#10671;

Power failures, which affect a whole neighborhood, not just your house, sometimes happen during a storm, or other times. Here are some things to remember in case you find yourself alone when this happens:

○ Call your parent or other adult to let him know what's happened. He may want you to call the electric company as well. (If the phone isn't working either, get to a neighbor's house if one is nearby. If not, handle the situation by yourself.)

○ If it's dark and you have to use candles or kerosene lamps, *be careful with them.* No time is a good time for a fire, but this is one of the *worst* times. Don't fool around! (Store candles in an easy-to-get-to spot so you won't have to stumble around in the dark to find them.)

○ If the heat goes off and you have a fireplace, be sure you know what you're doing before striking a match.

○ Don't open and close the refrigerator too much, and try not to open the freezer at all. Frozen foods will keep for quite a while without power, but not if you let in a lot of warm air.

○ Remember that blackouts usually don't last very long. Be patient and hang in there.

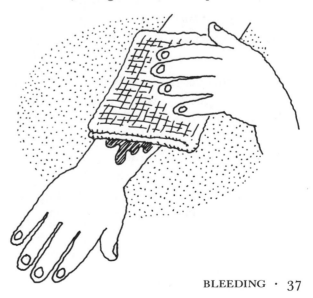

Finally, what you think is a blackout may only be a blown fuse, so check out ELECTRICAL PROBLEMS to find out how to handle that. It's a good idea to read it now; it may be difficult to see it in the dark.

◆ NOTES:

_____
_____
_____
_____

# ⮕ BLEEDING ⮐

## Be Direct

The best way to stop bleeding is to apply direct pressure to the wound. Even if it's serious, bleeding will almost always be stopped in this way. But it is important to act fast. So learn these simple steps:

**1. Hold a sterile gauze bandage right over the wound.** (In an emergency, use a very clean cloth, a piece of clothing, or just your hand.)

**2. Press down on the wound with your hand, keeping your fingers flat.** Don't let your fingers dig in.

**3. For bleeding on an arm or leg, hold the cut area up if possible.** Don't do this if it hurts the injured person, or if you think a bone might be broken.

**4. If the bleeding doesn't stop, add more gauze or cloth and keep pressing down on the wound.** Don't take off the first cloth to put on another.

5. If the wound is serious, give care for SHOCK, and get medical help fast.

BLEEDING · 37

## But Be Cautious

Don't use fluffy cotton to stop bleeding: it will stick to the cut. And don't use a *tourniquet* (a very tight band that cuts off all blood to an arm or leg) unless you have been trained to use it correctly. If you don't know what you're doing, it can do a lot more harm than good. Besides, direct pressure works almost every time.

If there's been an accident — even a minor one — and you see symptoms like coughed-up blood or vomited blood, call a doctor fast. This could mean that there's internal bleeding, and that needs immediate medical care.

See also FIRST AID.

▶ NOTES:

_____

_____

_____

_____

## ❧ BLENDERS/FOOD PROCESSORS ❧

You can make great things with a blender — but you can also make a great mess. If you *don't* want that to happen, follow these tips:

• *Don't* turn on the blender until the cover is firmly in place — unless you like cleaning banana milkshakes off the wall, the oven, the toaster, your sneakers . . .

• *Don't* fill the container to the top. At most, it should only be three-quarters full.

• *Don't* put *very hot* things into the container — especially if it's glass — it can break.

• *Don't* let the blender run for too long — a minute should be about enough for anything.

• *Don't* put anything — especially your fingers! — inside the container while the blender is running. If you *must* poke around inside, be sure the power is *off* by unplugging the blender.

The same rules apply to food processors. But these gadgets are more complicated than blenders, and more dangerous — if you don't know how to work them. If you use a processor, be very sure to read the instructions carefully, and to get some help from an adult until you're *sure* you understand what to do.

See also APPLIANCES.

◆ NOTES:

## ᕗ BOREDOM ᕗ

Some problems are not really problems, they're decisions. Take boredom (*please!!*). When you say you're bored, what you're really saying is that you're bored with yourself. So you have to decide what to do to make yourself unbored.

## What to Do, What to Do . . .

You have lots of choices:

- *Playing with a friend:* games, sports, cards, charades, whatever.
- *Playing alone:* puzzles, cut-outs, computer games, you-name-it.
- *Playing with a pet:* isn't it about time *you* learned to fetch the stick?
- *Watching television:* pick your programs well, and don't overdo it.
- *Reading:* books and magazines with adventure, mysteries, animal stories, puzzles, word games: everything in the world!
- *Writing letters:* you might even get some answers in the mail.
- *Cooking:* feed your family and friends (not to mention your enemies) with your very own homemade goodies.
- *Working on hobbies:* sports, arts and crafts, musical instruments, magic tricks.
- *Doing a favor:* run an errand, clean up the kitchen, teach your little brother to tell time.
- *Making things:* model planes, patches for your jeans, a dog house!
- *Exercising:* see the section on EXERCISE.

## It's Boring to Be Bored

No matter who you are or how old you are, there'll be times when something you've planned doesn't work out, and you'll have time on your hands. If you get into the habit of using that time to keep busy, you'll never be bored. You'll just decide whether to finish reading that book on U.F.O.'s, or make the model of the stegosaurus, or bake a batch of brownies, or . . . something else. If you decide to go around telling everyone that you have "nothing to do," you'll not only be bored, you'll be boring. Boring, *boring,* BORING!

## ❧ BREAKFAST IN BED ❧

### Please a Parent

One of the best ways to please a parent, and make up for some of the not-so-great things you've done lately, is to serve breakfast in bed. It's also a terrific gift, which you can present with a card like this:

```
┌─────────────────────────────────────┐
│                                     │
│  This is to announce that           │
│                                     │
│  ─────────────────────────────      │
│  (Your parent's name here)          │
│                                     │
│  is entitled to one                 │
│  BREAKFAST IN BED on                │
│  the day of his (her) choice        │
│  to be served by that               │
│  FAMOUS TERRIFIC CHEF               │
│                                     │
│  ─────────────────────────────      │
│  (Your name here)                   │
│                                     │
└─────────────────────────────────────┘
```

## What — and HOW!

To make this an event to remember (with joy), here are two things to think about:

- What to make
- How to serve it

What you make depends on what you know how to make. Don't decide on a fancy menu of French toast, sausage and melon if you've never fixed these things before. Choose foods you know how to do — bacon and eggs? Just eggs? Just bacon? And if you can hardly cook at all, you can serve something like juice, toast, and/or cereal with fruit and milk. Try to please your parent with some favorite dish — but almost everyone likes *something* that's easy to fix.

What *really* counts is how you serve it. First of all, it has to go on a tray, so get one out before you start. (It is no fun to have your wonderful breakfast ready, then spend ten minutes looking for a tray, while the eggs get cold and the juice gets warm.)

Be it ever so humble, breakfast in bed should look special. This may take a little planning, especially if the food itself is simple. Say you're just serving juice, toast, and coffee. Doesn't sound like much, does it? But you can put many little things on the tray that make it seem like much more — milk or cream, sugar, jams, jellies, or honey. Don't put containers like milk cartons on the tray; now is the time to use the good creamer or sugar bowl (unless they're very fragile). If possible, serve goodies like jam in little bowls or plates, not in their jars (unless the jars are small and pretty).

You can add fruit to almost any breakfast, which looks nice and is easy to do. Put fruit such as grapes, plums, pears on a cake plate, or slice up fruit, like a banana, and serve it in dessert bowls or stem glasses. If you have them, strawberries (with or without cream) are wonderful. And oranges or grapefruit, divided into sections, look very appetizing arranged on a small dish.

A really classy thing to do is to put a flower in a little vase on the tray. It can even be a paper flower (one you've made?), or a little buttercup from the lawn (if you've got a lawn — with butter-

cups). And for that final note of luxury, add the morning paper (or part of it). If the tray is getting crowded, bring the paper in separately.

How you bring in breakfast is also important. You should make a big production out of it, because, after all, it is a special occasion. But don't worry too much about getting everything perfect, especially the first time. Most people enjoy the idea of having breakfast in bed so much that they won't be very critical of your little mistakes.

See also COOKING.

 ॐ **BROKEN BONES** ॐ

### Is It Broken?

If someone has had an accident, and an injured part of the body doesn't look normal in shape, it's probably a broken bone. Don't be fooled if there isn't much

pain — sometimes the pain gets bad later. Only a doctor can tell for sure, usually with an X ray. But if you suspect a bone is broken, treat it as if it is. If it turns out that it's a sprain or a dislocation, you still will have taken the right steps.

### First Aid for Breaks

1. Call for an ambulance immediately.

2. Don't move the person unless there's danger — and don't move the injured part.

3. Keep the person lying down, calm, and quiet. (Be reassuring.)

4. If you're being taken by car to the doctor, try to support the broken part with a pillow or blanket.

5. Be on guard for SHOCK.

*Don't* try to put on a splint unless you've been trained to do this.

*Don't* try to straighten the limb or move the person in any way.

## Compound Fractures

*Fracture* is another word for *break*. A *compound* fracture is a break with broken skin. So, you have to give first aid for BLEEDING, too, while waiting for help to arrive. Use the direct pressure method, which simply means to press a sterile gauze bandage or a very clean cloth against the wound until the bleeding stops. But, since the bone is broken, you will have to be very careful not to press down too hard or to move the area where the break seems to be.

## Spine or Neck Injuries

These can be *really* serious, so be very careful not to move the person and to keep him/her warm and quiet until an ambulance arrives.

See also FIRST AID.

◆ NOTES:

_____
_____
_____
_____

## ❧ BROKEN DISHES/GLASS ❧

If something breakable breaks, and it's important to its owner — that expensive Chinese vase, someone's favorite coffee mug, a souvenir plate from Lake Wishi-Washi — and you suspect it's not too far gone to put the pieces back together, *carefully* pick up all the pieces (get every sliver you can) and put them away in a box or other container. If the pieces are sharp, wear gloves when picking them up. Tell your parent(s) about the accident and produce the pieces — maybe the object can be put back together.

If something breakable breaks, and it's an ordinary piece — a drinking glass or a plate — sweep all the pieces up com-

pletely (again, get every sliver), put them into a paper bag, and throw them away. If you think there are still tiny traces of glass, go over the area with dampened paper towels (throw them away, too). And mention it to your parent.

Be careful when you pick up glass: it can cut. And *never* vacuum up broken glass or china or dishes. The pieces can really mess up the vacuum cleaner, and then you'll have two things to explain to your parent(s).

See also SPILLS, STAINS, CUTS AND SCRAPES, and SPLINTERS — if necessary.

## ❧ BROTHERS AND SISTERS ❧

*"How come he always gets to do it?"*

*"I'm just not talking to him anymore!"*

*"If she's going to stay, so am I!"*

*"I'm drawing a line across the room. And you just better not cross it!"*

*"It's your turn to take out the garbage."*

*"She never has to do anything!"*

Welcome to the world of brothers and sisters. Even if you only have one, there are bound to be hassles. That's because whenever you get more than one person in the same place for any length of time, whether they're related or not, they just can't agree on everything. Since you really don't want to run away from home, and the problem won't go away, here are some ideas on how to live with it.

### Sibling Rivalry

You've heard the term, and probably know that it means competition (rivalry) between children within the same family (siblings). Oh, boy, do you know what it means. And the thing is, it's perfectly normal.

You want love and attention from your parents, but so do your siblings. So you end up sharing your parents' attention (sometimes along with your room, a telephone, some games, and who knows what else). So you feel jealous or hostile, and no wonder. Just don't let it get the best of you, and keep the arguing/fighting down to a minimum. You'll find you get more of what you want, more of the time, if you can get your siblings on your side, than if you act as if you're enemies. When the two (or three or ten?) of you get together and present your case to your folks, there's a better chance of getting them to say yes, than if all of you are starting World War III over some dumb detail.

Sometimes, this just isn't possible. You may feel as if your parents are always siding with your brother. Or that they're constantly comparing you to him. If your dad says, "Why can't you be neat like your brother?" you probably will feel angry at your dad *and* your brother. After all, your brother may be neat, but he's not perfect. *He* failed his history test. And you didn't. It's not fair!

Nope. It isn't. But your dad isn't perfect, either, and maybe he didn't stop to think about how that statement made you feel. And maybe he doesn't realize he's not paying enough attention to your side of things. Before you go beating up on your brother, or picking on him, or making fun of him in front of his friends, or doing whatever you do to get even, try to cool down. Then talk to your dad, or your mom, or both. It might help. Even if it

doesn't work the first time, don't give up. You don't always listen to good advice the first time you hear it, and neither do other people. Give them a chance.

The same goes for complaints about having to do more than your share of the chores, or not getting enough clothes, or allowance, or attention. If you imagine yourself as the parent, you can see how hard it is to be perfectly fair about everything. So give everybody a break: if things are not exactly the way you'd like them to be, stick up for your rights, but don't expect miracles.

## Sharing

Whether it's a room or a set of Chinese checkers, sharing can be a problem. There's Big Trouble if:

- You're neat, your sister isn't.
- You like to read at night, your brother doesn't.
- You want to hang up pictures of rock stars and your brother hates them.
- You like to share your things but your sister insists she be asked about everything — even touching her pencil sharpener!

Then, too, the problem may not be with your parents, but with your brother or sister. The child may feel hurt when you

go off alone, especially because (since you're older) you get to do more things. The way to handle this is to give him/her more time when you're home together (a little attention goes a long way), and then try to take him/her with you as a special treat from time to time.

And don't be alarmed if a younger sibling starts imitating you. Your little broth-

ers and sisters "look up to you" not just because you're taller and they actually have to tilt their heads back to look up, but also because you're older and they see you as a model. It may get on your nerves to hear them imitating you — using your expressions, trying to dress or even walk like you. But it's actually a compliment, so try to see it that way.

## "You're Too Young to _____"

What? Stay up late? Go out with friends? Have your own record player? If you're younger, you may feel as though your older sister or brother gets to do *everything,* and you can't do *anything.* It is true that the older you are the more you do, but that works two ways. Older kids have more privileges, like staying out later at night. But they also have to do things like finding a summer job, doing more schoolwork, or helping out around the house more often. Also, remind yourself that you probably get to do more than your older brothers or sisters did when they were your age. Parents tend to be stricter with their first child, and easier on the younger ones.

But if you think you're being ignored or neglected, or are underprivileged, then speak up. And try to show that you can be a responsible person. Whatever you do, don't mope around and make a nuisance of yourself. That will make you seem more like the baby in the family.

Drawing a line down the middle of your room just won't work. And threatening "to tell Mom if . . . " won't do much for your relationship. Instead, try making a list of your problems and ask your roommate to do the same. Choose the things that bug you the most and star them. These are the things to work out first. Then try to strike a bargain, with each side giving a little and taking a little. Be fair: if your brother agrees to let you read at night, you could take down four Bruce Springsteen posters. And if you need more help on the subject, check out the section on PRIVACY.

## "Stop That Fighting!"

As we've said, it's better for brothers and sisters to stick together, than to become unglued and attack each other. But when you do become angry, try to follow the

rules for arguing (yes, there are rules, and we tell you about them in the section on ARGUMENTS). Sometimes, you have to bring in a parent as an umpire, but avoid "tattling" — it breeds mistrust.

## "You're Older, So_____"

Fill in the blank. If you are the oldest, you'll have no trouble. It could be: a) "You ought to know better," or, b) "Let her have her way this time," or, c) "You can do more than he can," or, d) all of the above.

Sometimes, you have a real injustice on your hands. Your little sister may not be all that innocent, and takes advantage of your mother's belief that she is. If this happens, talk it over with your mom or dad. The worst thing is to say nothing and take it out on your sister. Then you'll be in more trouble with your folks.

You also may have to take a younger brother or sister with you when you'd rather go someplace alone. If it happens because your parents simply don't realize how annoying it is, you may be able to work something out. But they may not be able to afford a babysitter all the time, and you'll have to take on this responsibility more often than you'd like.

## In the Middle

Some people think you're lucky to be a middle child, because you don't have the problems of being either the oldest or the youngest. But others see it this way: the middle child is older than the youngest, and younger than the oldest, and so has the problems of both! What can we say? Well, it's always better to look on the bright side, so why not take the attitude that you're at an advantage? You can learn from your older siblings, and be looked up to by your younger ones.

## Babying the Baby

It's not unusual to feel really excited before a new baby comes, then depressed after it arrives. Before, the anticipation is building up, with everyone wondering if it'll be a boy or a girl, waiting for the big day. Then, all of a sudden, the baby is home, and it doesn't seem to care about *you* at all. *And* it's getting all the attention, not only from your immediate family, but from your neighbors and other relatives. *And* your parents may be grouchy more of the time, especially after a night or two of staying up with a crying infant. *And* you have to change your life around a little, like not playing your records or TV so loudly, and tiptoeing around at certain times.

No matter what happens, remember that your parents love you just as much as they did before the baby was born. But taking care of a newborn infant is incredibly time-consuming. That's why your folks are so preoccupied. You may even find that a younger brother or sister begins acting more like a baby, too, in an effort to get more attention. And that doesn't help matters.

In spite of all this, getting to know a newborn infant can be a wonderful experience. And you're in a great position. Let's face it: your parents have most of the responsibility, while you have all the pleasure. You can be there when the baby giggles and coos, says its first word, smiles at you and says your name, and later, begins to walk. There's something so delicious about babies that they make people feel good just to look at them. And you are there to share this enjoyment. Make the most of the opportunity while you can, and, to help you through the rough spots, read about INFANTS.

## The Only Child

If you're an only child, and you've read this section, you may be counting your blessings. But if you wish you had brothers and sisters because your problem is being alone too much of the time, the sections on BOREDOM and LONELINESS may give you some help.

## ✌ BRUISES ✌

Bruises are those black and blue (and red and purple and yellow) marks that appear after a blow, bump, bang, or knock. The reason for all those strange colors is bleeding under the skin. There's not much you can do for it, except wait for the color to fade away (count on ten to fourteen days).

If the bruise is painful or swollen, apply an ice pack for a half hour at a time every couple of hours for twenty-four hours. Later, when the color really comes out, warm, wet towels may help it to fade a little faster.

If there's a bruise and the skin is broken, treat it as a cut (see CUTS AND SCRAPES).

## Budgeting

See ALLOWANCE.

# Bumps

See BRUISES and HEAD INJURIES.

# ✎ BURNS ✎

A burn feels hot, right? So the first thing you do is cool it down — by soaking it in very cold water. (Don't use ice, though, because it can stick to the burn.)

Look at the burn to see what kind it is:

*First degree* will be red and painful.

*Second degree* will also have blisters and swelling.

*Third degree* will be even worse (skin may be insensitive or charred).

You do this to figure out how bad the burn is. A second-degree burn is more serious than a first-degree burn, and will need medical care. If it's even worse — a third-degree burn — get medical help *immediately*. (Even first-degree burns, when on the face or near the eyes, need to be seen by a doctor. And some burns are *mixed* — they may be mostly first degree, with second degree near the point that received the most heat. All these mixed-type burns should be seen by a professional.)

Put a sterile gauze bandage or a very clean cloth on the burn to keep out dirt. But make the dressing loose, so it won't stick to blisters. And tell your parents about the burn, even if it's minor.

See also FIRST AID, and EYE INJURIES, if the burn is in or near the eye.

▸ NOTES:

_____
_____
_____
_____
_____

# Buses

See PUBLIC TRANSPORTATION.

*Just*

# ɔ CAMP ɞ

## The Right Camp for the Right Kid

Every camp is a little different, and that's a good thing, because all kids are different, too. If you're going to camp, you may not have any choice about which one. Your parents may have a favorite, your school or church may offer a special arrangement for you, a particular camp may be the only one your family can afford, or whatever. But if you *do* have something to say about it, here are some things to think about:

• What are your special interests: crafts, arts, sports, music?

• Do you want a coed camp, or one that's just for boys or just for girls?

• Do you want a good, all-purpose camp, or one of the special types, such as those that help you to lose weight, to play tennis, or to learn about nature.

One way to find out about camps is to ask people about the ones they've been to. The older brothers and sisters of your friends are a good bet. They have experience. You can also call the American Camping Association, or ask at your local YMCA/YWCA, church, temple, youth center, school, or Boy/Girl Scout troop.

## Day or (Over)Night?

If you have a choice, think about whether you'd rather go to a day camp or a sleep-away camp. Here are some facts to help you decide. They'll also give you some idea of what to expect if you already know you're going to camp.

*DAY CAMP*
Usually, you're picked up in the morning by a bus with lots of other kids, and are brought home in the late afternoon on the same bus. Sometimes, parents form car pools to take kids to camp.

*Gear:* Before your first day, the camp will probably give you a list of things you should wear or take with you each day. The list will look something like this:

| | | |
|---|---|---|
| 1 bathing suit | 1 pair shorts | Sneakers |
| 1 bathing cap | 1 pair jeans | Socks |
| 2 towels | 1 sweater | Brush or comb |
| | Gym bag (to hold all this stuff) | |

*All in a Day's Camping:* You usually have a general counselor who's in charge of one group of kids, all about your age. That counselor will take you to special activities, like swimming or horseback riding, where there'll be other counselors who are experts in these things. A typical day might include things like swimming, arts and crafts, baseball (or softball, or soccer, or basketball), tennis, singing, and eating.

## OVERNIGHT CAMP
*Don't Forget the Flashlight!:* Most sleep-away camps have a season that's about eight weeks long. You may be staying there anywhere from one week to the full two months. So how much you take with you depends on how long you're going to stay. Usually, the camp will send you a list. For a four-week stay, it might be:

Some camps may also ask you to bring along sheets, pillowcases, and a sleeping bag. And everything has to be clearly marked or labeled with your name. Pack all your things in a trunk or large suitcase. *Don't* use any valuable luggage.

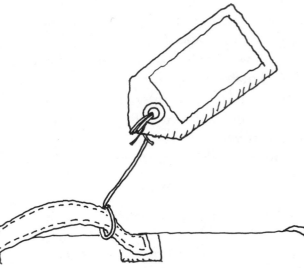

2 bathing suits
4 towels
3 pairs pajamas (2 heavy, 1 light)
1 terry-cloth bathrobe
1 pair slippers
8 pairs underwear
8 pairs socks
4 pairs shorts
4 pairs jeans
1 sweatshirt

1 or 2 sweaters
4 long-sleeved shirts
6 or 8 T-shirts
1 pair sneakers
1 pair hiking boots
1 pair riding boots
1 raincoat
1 warm jacket
Toothbrush, toothpaste, and plastic cup
2 bars soap and soap dish

Brush and comb
1 (plastic) bottle shampoo
Address book
Stationery
Stamps, pens, postcards
Musical instrument (if you play one)
Books, small games
Insect repellent
Flashlight (with extra batteries)

*What Not to Pack:* Camps have plenty of their own animals, so this is *not* the time to take your pet guppies (even if they are cute). You also do *not* need: jewelry, blow-dryers, good clothing, food, matches, large amounts of money.

*Cubbies and Buddies:* Your room at camp will not be like your room at home. It's either a tent, or — more likely — a cabin with bunk beds. There's a small amount of shelf space called "cubbies," which you share with up to ten other campers and two counselors. That's why you have to think twice about bringing everything you own with you: there may be no place to put it.

Sharing like this can be fun, but it can also mean problems, like arguments, or selfish people who take too much space or make noise when you're trying to sleep. But most kids find that there's more good than bad about camping. Even those who are scared about going usually end up liking it. A lot. It's like a slumber party or sleeping over at a friend's — a special vacation, just for kids.

*Homesicknesses: Causes and Cures:* So if it's so great, then why do you sometimes find a tear or two making its way down your cheek? Unless you've been peeling onions, you're probably homesick.

Don't worry. This happens to almost everyone: at camp, or, when you're older, at college, or at the army base, or in a strange city where you've just got a new job. Homesickness is an overall rotten feeling that's hard to explain. But the things that bring it on are usually quite clear. You just lost a game, or you're not enjoying some of the activities, or you've had a fight with one of your bunkmates, or you're feeling lonely, or you've got a cold or a stomachache. These are all problems you might have at home. The difference is that when you're in familiar surroundings, problems don't seem so bad, and you have old friends and your family to help you.

But wait. You're not exactly alone at camp, you know. Okay, you miss your folks. But there are lots of other kids (and some of them may be homesick, too). The best cure for homesickness is to talk it over with someone. The worst thing to do is suffer in silence.

Campers have also found that two other things help: one is keeping busy. It is very hard to be miserable when you're hitting a tennis ball or swimming across a lake. The feeling of homesickness will pass no matter what you do (or don't do). But it will pass faster if you're active.

The other cure is writing a letter. Not quite as good as talking face-to-face, but it helps. The only trouble with this is that when you're feeling really low, you tend to make things sound worse (*much* worse) than they are. By the time you mail the letter, you may even be feeling a little better. And by the time your parents (or whomever you sent it to) get the letter, you might be fine. But they don't know this, and can get very upset. So, think twice before you write a letter like this:

I'm going to DIE if I have to stay in this rotten place another second.
I can't stand it!
They're trying to POISON me with this Yechhy food!!!

Your parents may take you on your word, and come to save you from a fate worse than death. Meanwhile, your homesickness is a thing of the past, and the last thing in the world you want to do is leave the camp!

*Visits and Phone Calls (or, Letters Are Better):* If you're really homesick, and even if you aren't, you'll probably like Visitors' Day. Most camps have them about halfway through the season — the end of the first month.

Most camps don't have visiting if you're staying for a shorter time. And they don't encourage phone calls, either. This is partly because of the cost: think of the phone bill! But camps have also found that letters are better (that's why you should take an address book and paper with you). You stay in touch with your family and friends, but you don't depend on them so much that way.

## The Rule about Rules

All camps have rules. Things like:

- No Running near the Pool
- Always Swim with a Buddy
- Stay in the Shallow Water until You've Passed Your Swimming Test

It's easy to see that these rules are made for your safety. Some others might be harder to take, but there are reasons for them. For example, most camps have a rule against having candy on the grounds. Maybe you've heard the song, "The ants go marching one by one . . ." Well, at camp, they march one hundred by one hundred. And if there are sweet foods around, it gets worse. You won't starve, though. You get three meals a day — simple, basic food, nothing fancy. And there's sometimes a canteen where you can get snacks between meals.

If you don't want to spend more time in hot water than you do in the cool pool, learn the rules and do your best to follow them. If you don't understand something, ask questions.

It's really a tough life: swimming, hiking, singing, snacking, giggling, and pillow fighting. Are you *sure* you want to go?

# Children

See BROTHERS AND SISTERS, INFANTS, BABYSITTING, and ENTERTAINING CHILDREN.

  ## CHOKING

If the choking doesn't seem that bad, encourage the person to cough. It could be that a piece of food is stuck, and the coughing could make it come out. But if that doesn't work, or if the person is gasping, having trouble breathing or talking, and turning very pale (even blue!), use the Heimlich Maneuver — right away!

The Heimlich Maneuver is a technique invented by a doctor to save choking victims. It's not complicated, and you can learn to do it. But don't try it in an emergency unless you know what you're doing. Read this section and study the illustrations, then practice with a friend — that'll help you remember the technique in case you ever need it.

1. Get behind the person and wrap your arms around his/her waist. (If the person is sitting, go behind the chair and do the same thing.)

2. Put your fist, thumb side in, against the person's abdomen — just above the navel, just below the rib cage.

3. With your other hand, grasp your fist and pull it into the person's abdomen with a quick, upward thrust.

4. Repeat this movement a few more times if you have to.

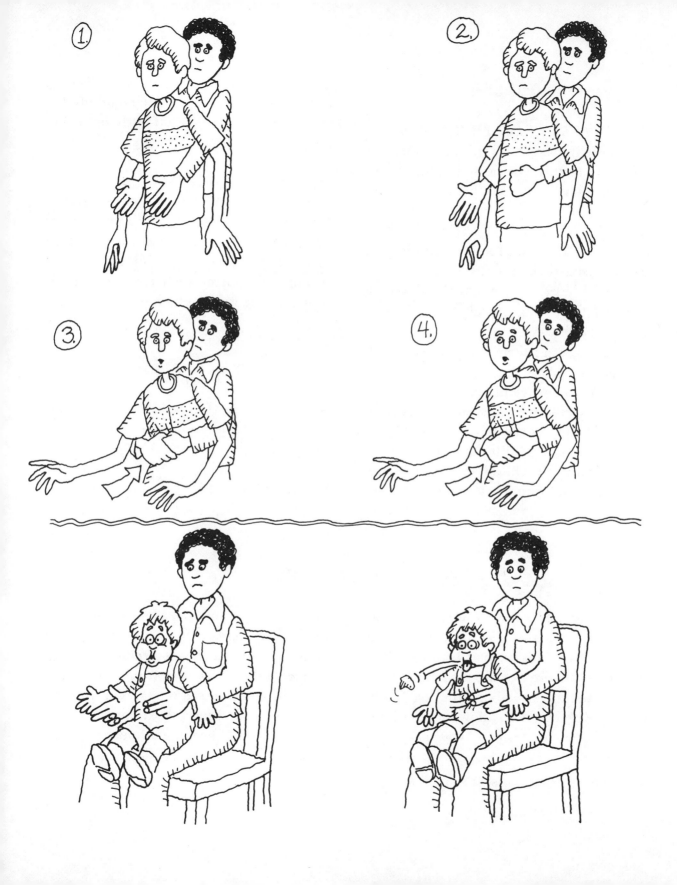

## Special Cases

*IF THE PERSON IS LYING DOWN*
The basic movement is still the same. But you have to turn the person onto his/her back and kneel over his/her hips.

*IF THE VICTIM IS AN INFANT*
Before you try the Heimlich Maneuver, try four sharp slaps between the baby's shoulder blades. This might shake loose a piece of food that's stuck there, just as coughing does.

If that doesn't work, use the Heimlich Maneuver. Follow the same basic steps for an infant as you would for an adult, except that you sit the child on your lap, and you use your fingers, not your fist. Place the index and middle fingers of both hands against the child's abdomen (again, above the navel and below the rib cage).

Press with a quick, upward thrust. Repeat a few times if necessary. You could also do the maneuver with the infant lying down, face upward.

*IF* YOU *ARE CHOKING*
If no one is there to help you, press your fist into your abdomen with your other hand, with quick, upward thrusts. Or lean forward and press your abdomen over a strong, solid object, such as a piece of furniture or the back of a chair.

## In Any Case

After the rescue, the person should *always* see a doctor, even though the choking has stopped.

See also FIRST AID.

## CHORES

A chore can be a bore. Or it can be a way of learning something, earning something, or both. Most kids have at least one daily or weekly chore to do: anything from milking the cow to walking the dog. Sometimes, you get paid an allowance for doing your chores, sometimes you get extra money for each of your chores, and sometimes "payment" is knowing that you're helping your family get along.

A chore *won't* be a bore if you see the value of what you're doing. You may be learning something like taking care of young children, keeping a house in order, caring for a pet. You can get to be really good at these things and that feels good. Besides, you'll get experience in judging how long something will take, figuring out the best time to do it, and knowing when to quit and when to stick to it. These are skills that can make you better at all sorts

of things: schoolwork, sports, music, dancing . . . almost anything. You can even make a chore into a "game" by trying to guess how long it will take or trying to do it faster than the last time.

A chore *will* be a bore when you put it off so long that you have to give up some-

thing fun in order to get it done. And it's really a drag when you're constantly nagged about not doing it.

For information on how to handle certain chores, see the sections on BED-MAKING, CLEANING HOUSE, COOKING, DISHES, EN-TERTAINING CHILDREN, FOOD SHOPPING, LAUNDRY, PET CARE, and PLANT CARE.

◆ NOTES:

```
_____
_____
_____
_____
_____
_____
```

# Circuit Breakers

See ELECTRICAL PROBLEMS.

# ✍ CLEANING HOUSE ✍

## Keep It Straight

One way to avoid having to straighten up so often is to do your part to keep it neat in the first place. This means not dropping things, one by one, until they've formed an Olympic obstacle course. One good week of "I don't have time to clean up" can mean you'll need a bulldozer instead of a broom to get it back in order.

Of course, you're not the only person who lives in your house, and everyone slips up now and then. So, when company's coming and you're asked to clean up the house, you should know how to handle it in a hurry. "Cleaning up" (or "straightening up" or "neatening up" — take your choice) usually means doing things like dusting, sweeping, throwing away old newspapers, clearing off tables, emptying ashtrays, hanging up clothing, doing dishes, or fluffing up pillows. It usually does *not* mean heavy-duty cleaning like

waxing floors or washing walls and windows.

## The Order of Things

Figure it out. Dumping a half-empty garbage can before you've picked up in the living room doesn't make sense. The can will fill up as you straighten up, and you'll have to empty it again. It's the same with dishes. If you do the ones in the sink first, before you go through the rubble in the playroom, you may end up doing a second load — the glasses, plates, and spoons you found under old magazines. Every family has its own sense of order, but here are two more tips:

- *Start at the top.* Clean top shelves before you do the lower ones, and clean tabletops before you do the floor. Small things — and dust — fall as you stir things up. So when you finish at the bottom, you're getting all the mess cleaned up.
- *Always sweep the floors before you wash them.* Otherwise, you end up washing the dust.

## More on Floors

For a clean sweep, it's usually better to move things out of the way, rather than trying to sweep around them. Of course, you can't push out the sofa, but you can get small chairs and tables out of the way. Then, start at a back corner of the room and sweep toward the front, making a pile of dust as you go. Have a dustpan ready for the finish, then dump all the dirt in the garbage. For cleaning rugs, see the section on VACUUM CLEANERS.

## The Must on Dust

As with sweeping, it's better to move things before you dust than to dust around them. Put everything to one side of a surface, dust the other side, then move the stuff and dust the rest. Or, put everything somewhere else until you've dusted the whole thing. Don't use a totally dry cloth: it doesn't get rid of the dust, it just moves it around. You can dampen the cloth slightly with plain old water for many things, but you might want to use furniture polish or oil on wood. Ask a parent. Try to be as thorough as possible, and to cheat as little as possible. ("They'll never *look* under that big book, so why should I *dust* under it?")

## Heavy-Duty Cleaning

Bathrooms and kitchens need to be cleaned with strong products, such as ammonia or disinfectants, and everyone does it differently. If you have a job like this, get very specific instructions from your parents, and do it their way.

▸ NOTES:

_____

_____

_____

_____

_____

# Clothes

See CLOTHING CARE, IRONING, and LAUNDRY.

## ✺ CLOTHING CARE ✺

### Let It All Hang Up

The first rule of clothing care is simply to hang things up. Your clothes last longer, look better, and don't have to be cleaned or washed so often.

How you arrange them in your closet is up to you. Some people are fanatically neat about this. (They are known as "closet cases.") They arrange their clothes by type: the shirts and blouses, skirts and trousers, suits and dresses. Others separate their closets into casual, school, and dress-up clothes. There is even one person who hangs clothes in the closet by color: all the reds together, all the blues, all the whites, all the yellows . . .

Find a system that works for you — and use it. Even no system at all can be a system, if you're happier that way. But do hang things up, and do be neat. Put the pants on the hangers so the seams and creases line up, and button a few buttons on shirts so they stay on the hangers.

### But Drawers Go in the Drawers

The same is true for the way you arrange and keep your dresser drawers. You'll probably want to sort things out by type: socks there, T-shirts over there, underwear here. Resist the temptation to crumble things up and throw them in any old drawer. You'll pay for it later, with messy shirts and missing socks.

### Clean Clothes

Attack stains (CHARGE!) as quickly as possible, before they "set" and become hard (or impossible) to remove. To find out how, read the section on STAINS. And if you're doing the wash, read the section on LAUNDRY. Read the labels carefully to find out what to do, and be on the lookout for tags that say *Dry Clean Only*. Putting something like that in the washing machine is a sure way to end a beautiful relationship with your favorite piece of clothing. Bye, pants!

## Patch It Up

Clothing sometimes has to be repaired: a button needs sewing on, a hem needs letting out. Doing these things is not difficult, but it would be difficult to give you step-by-step instructions for all the little sewing jobs you could encounter. (These are called "Clothes Encounters of the Thread Kind.") Even if you've got a willing parent to do it for you, it's good to know some basic sewing, so you won't be

helpless when you get a split seam and there's no one around to help. You also might enjoy learning how to put patches on your jeans — just for the fun of it. Whatever you do, don't throw away something that's perfectly good just because it needs a minor repair.

## Shoe-In

Shoes are special, and need special care. From time to time, leather shoes and boots should be cleaned with a leather restorer or saddle soap to keep them looking healthy. If your shoes or boots get wet, take them off as soon as you get home. Stuff them with crumpled newspaper (roughly into the shape of your feet) and let them dry out *naturally*. Don't put them near the radiator, into the oven (you wouldn't!), or under a hairdryer.

Sneakers need attention, too. They should be washed when they need it. When is that? Let your eyes (and nose) be your guide. Yes, you can throw them into the washing machine and dryer, if it's okay with your folks, but throw in a few towels, too, so they won't wake up the dead with their shake, rattle, and roll.

# Colds and Flu

See ILLNESS.

# ☙ COOKING ❧

## What's Cooking?

*The Official Kids' Survival Kit* is *not* a cookbook. So if you're looking for loads of recipes, you'd be better off using one of the many fine cookbooks around, some of

which are even written just for kids. The purpose of this book is to help you survive, and that means knowing how to fix yourself a good, easy meal or snack.

Good and easy. You probably know quite a few things that fit that description. Let's see now: there's peanut-butter sandwiches. Then there's . . . peanut-butter sandwiches. And, oh, yes, that old favorite, peanut-butter sandwiches! Okay, what's the joke? That most kids love peanut-butter sandwiches. And the funny thing is, they're pretty good for you, too. For one thing, peanut butter has a fair amount of protein (yeah, protein!). And if you use whole-grain or bran bread, you even get some roughage (also known as "fiber"), which is, as you've probably heard, good for you, too.

Other things that are also good and easy include: cereal (but not the kind loaded with sugar), yogurt, cheese, nuts, raisins, and any kind of fresh fruit. (For a more detailed list, see *Round-the-Clock "Cooking,"* later in this section.) As you can see, you don't actually have to cook any of these things, and you practically don't have to do any work. Okay, they haven't invented a banana with an automatic zipper. But they're working on it, they're working on it.

Even though you like raisins or apples or cheese, and you have no trouble making yourself a snack, you can become confused when you have to put a meal together. No

sweat. There are ways to make really simple meals, and you can learn how. No, you wouldn't want to eat them all the time. You'd get homesick for the kinds of food that *do* take lots of time and trouble to make — like stews and roasts and fancy sauces and pies and cakes and *stop!* Let's get back to basics and talk about some in-a-pinch meals you can handle. But first, two words of warning:

☞ *Warning #1:* You may already know how to boil water and toast toast. But if you don't, or if you're unsure about working the oven, the range, the blender, or even the electric can opener, now's the time to learn how. Quick! Read the section on APPLIANCES and *Common Sense in the Kitchen* on page 3, before you waste away to a shadow of your former self. . . .

☞ *Warning #2:* You may also know about the dangers of food poisoning, which comes from eating things that have "gone bad." So, if you notice that any food looks or smells strange — such as bread with mold on it, canned soup with a "different" aroma, meat that's a little green around the edges — or if you're at all suspicious, DON'T EAT IT.

## Breakfast, Kid Style

Yes, it is an important meal. But it doesn't have to be that big a deal. It's better to eat something — even that famous peanut-butter sandwich — than nothing at all.

But here are some other easy breakfasts for a change of pace.

## THE OFFICIAL PRACTICALLY-NO-WORK BASIC BREAKFAST

A glass of fruit juice (orange, grapefruit, pineapple, prune, apple, etc.)

Toast with butter (whole-grain or bran bread is best)

A glass of milk

You can add things to this basic breakfast, but you have to do a little more work.

| WHAT TO ADD | WHAT TO DO |
| --- | --- |
| 1 soft-boiled egg | Gently place an egg in a small saucepan with enough water in it to cover the egg. Put it over medium heat, and when the water boils begin timing it: three minutes for an egg that's hard on the outside, runny on the inside. Experiment with timing until you get it exactly the way you like it, but in the beginning it's better to overcook it (you may get a hard-boiled egg!) than to undercook it (you'll get a runny mess). For more on eggs, see page 72. |
| 1 bowl of hot (or cold) cereal | For hot cereal, follow the directions on the package. Most instant cereals need boiling water and stirring. |

You can also change the basic breakfast by substituting half a grapefruit for the fruit juice. This means you have to slice the grapefruit open and cut out the sections, which is hard to describe in writing, but fairly easy to do. If you love (or are even mildly attracted to) grapefruits, get someone to teach you how. Of course, you can always cut it in half, then in quarters, and eat it like an orange. (A fresh orange is also a good substitute for the juice.)

The toast can be English muffin, corn or bran muffin, raisin toast, cinnamon toast, or even a quick grilled-cheese sandwich — made in the oven or the toaster oven with slices of cheese on bread or a muffin.

## Lunch and Light Dinners, the Easy Way

Remember, you just want to get some good-tasting, nourishing food into your grumbling stomach. These meals are not recommended for a formal dinner party, or for every day. The point is, you don't have to be helpless — or hungry — when you're on your own in the kitchen.

## THE OFFICIAL PRACTICALLY-NO-WORK BASIC LUNCH AND LIGHT-DINNER MENUS

*Meal #1: Soup and Sandwiches:* The soup makes it a hot meal, and together the

two make you feel that you've eaten something substantial, not just a snack.

*The Soup.* Use canned, frozen, or packaged soup mixes, and follow the directions carefully. For example, some canned soups need water added, some don't. If you weren't paying attention, you could end up with *very* watery broth or *very* thick split-pea soup.

You can get a little fancy, and add little touches such as grated cheese, chopped onion, or parsley to prepared soup to make it taste and look better. Try spices such as onion salt, dill, or oregano — sparingly, until you find out which ones you like in which soups. But you don't have to do anything special if you don't want to. Just wait till it's soup yet, and serve.

*The Sandwich.* It can be ever so humble. A single slice of cheese between two pieces of thin bread makes a sandwich, we suppose. But come on, live a little. Create sandwiches with interesting combinations of whatever's around. (This is known as The Leftover Sandwich Maneuver.) Even if you use only one kind of meat — either the kind made especially for sandwiches, or pieces of last night's chicken, roast, or ham — don't be stingy with the filling. You can make salad for sandwiches from tuna fish, chicken, ham, turkey, shrimp, or hard-boiled eggs, by breaking or cutting up the pieces and mixing with mayonnaise. Add chopped celery, onion, parsley, or tomatoes, if you like.

To finish off your sandwich (before you really finish it off), spread the bread with *something*. Some people like butter and/or mayonnaise or mustard, or Russian dressing, or all of the above. Just don't leave the bread high and dry.

To make the sandwich look nice on the plate — and more like a "real" meal — add something colorful. Something colorful? Like a balloon? What do you mean? We mean that simple foods, like soup and sandwiches, can look really appetizing if they're presented well. The colorful things you add (they're called *garnishes,* if you want to get fancy about it) could be slices of tomato or hard-boiled eggs, olives (black, green, or both), pickles, peppers,

parsley, carrot sticks. If you make soup and sandwiches this way — prepared well and served up with a little dash — you'll feel as if you've had a good meal. And you have. Add a glass of milk and a dessert, and it will feel like a feast.

## Meal #2: Hamburger "Steak" and Salad

The Menu: Hamburger
          Salad
          Bread and butter
          Milk
          Dessert

You can add vegetables, such as canned or frozen peas or string beans. But don't have potatoes if you're planning to have cake, pie, or cookies for dessert — too many carbohydrates. (Potatoes take too much time for this kind of meal, anyway.)

*The Hamburger.* To make a hamburger, you make a patty out of about ¼ pound of ground beef, and fry it on the stove or broil it in the oven. Now this sounds easy, and it is, once you get the hang of it. But don't try it out for the first (or maybe even second or third) time alone. What could happen? You could cook it too fast and burn it, or splatter fat all over, or even start a fire. But if you learn how, you can do it quickly and safely in about ten minutes.

Most people like the way burgers taste when they add seasonings and a few other ingredients to the ground beef. Salt and pepper, for sure. Chopped-up onion or parsley, if you like them. Grated cheese, Worcestershire, soy, or steak sauce, mustard, even a raw egg are all things you'll find in many well-bred burgers. And you thought it was all meat!

*The Salad.* Unless you're really speedy, better get the salad ready before you put the hamburger on to cook. Then you won't have to worry about burning the burger while you're tossing and turning. What's in a salad? Almost anything you'd like. But to make this a balanced meal, start with some lettuce, then add things like tomato, onion, cucumber, peppers. If you like bacon bits or slices of hard-boiled eggs, even cottage cheese or pieces of tuna fish, and you have these things, by all means add them. You'll have to cut up some of these ingredients, so be careful.

Use a ready-made salad dressing, if you like. Or make a simple one yourself with oil and vinegar (or lemon juice). Just mix a few tablespoons of oil with a tablespoon of vinegar (or lemon juice), add a dash of salt, pepper, and other spices if you like, and stir well. Pour it over the salad and toss. By the way, a super salad — filled with pieces of meat, fish, cheese, and eggs — can be a meal in itself.

*What's for Dessert?* The best and easiest thing is fruit. You can make any fruit look fancier, and more like dessert, by slicing it up and serving it in a bowl or glass. Add a topping such as cream or whipped cream or even chocolate syrup to bananas; or honey to peaches or strawberries.

What else? Cake, cookies, or ice cream are okay for this meal. (Ice cream even has some protein in it — hooray again!) Just don't make the dessert bigger than the main course.

## Round-the-Clock "Cooking"

Some foods can be eaten just about any-time. And sometimes you're not that hungry, even if the clock says it's time for dinner. We've mentioned some of these foods earlier as snacks or breakfast foods. But there's no reason you can't have them for lunch or dinner, sometimes.

*THE OFFICIAL NO-COOKING-NEEDED BASIC ANYTIME FOODS*
*Fruits and Nuts.* Fresh is best, but frozen and canned are okay, too. And don't forget applesauce. Besides fruits like apples, peaches, plums, nectarines, bananas, oranges, grapefruit, cherries, and berries, try dried fruit like raisins, prunes, apricots, or dates.

*Cereal with Milk.* The best kinds are things like shredded wheat, and other natural-type cereals. The worst (and definitely not recommended) have a lot of sugar, and artificial flavors like chocolate. Add fruit if you like.

*Cheese and Crackers.* You can fix quite a "spread" with just a little spreading.

*Ice Cream and Other Goodies.* Not too often or too much, and only if you're getting enough of the other foods you need.

*Leftovers.* Snacking or light meals doesn't have to mean junk foods. When you're a little hungry, a piece of leftover meat, soup, vegetable, or salad can hit the spot. Warning: don't touch that chicken if you know its fate is to be served in a casserole for tonight's dinner.

And let us not forget the ever-popular ... *Peanut-Butter Sandwich*(!) Make it fancier if you want by adding a little honey and some pieces of cut-up orange. Okay, okay, jelly is all right, too.

Some foods need a little cooking, but they're worth it. So here it is . . .

### THE OFFICIAL HARDLY-ANY-COOKING BASIC ANYTIME FOODS

At the top of the list comes the inexpensive, almost-always-in-the-refrigerator, full-of-protein-and-other-good-things food:

*The Egg.* You've already heard about the soft-boiled egg in the breakfast section.

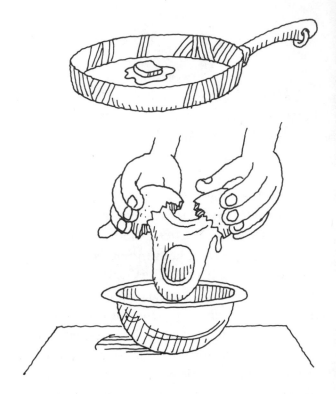

To make it *hard-boiled,* just cook it a little longer — about ten minutes after the boil.

Fried eggs are made with a frying pan (that figures!), a little butter or margarine, and a spatula. Melt the butter over low heat. Crack the eggshell and drop the egg (gently) into a small bowl or cup. (After a while, you'll get so good at this that you'll do it directly into the frying pan, but that takes a little practice.) Try not to get any pieces of shell mixed in with the egg, and try not to break the yolk. If you do break the yolk, it's not a disaster, it just won't look as nice. If you get any pieces of shell in the egg, lift them out with a spoon be-

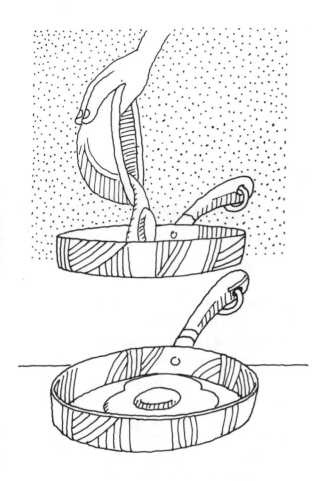

and onto the plate, with the help of the spatula.

Scrambled eggs are not made in a scrambling pan. (Smart aleck.) You use a frying pan and butter, same as for fried eggs. The difference is that you beat up the eggs in a bowl, add salt, pepper, and a little milk, cream, or water, depending on your taste, then cook them in the melted butter. You can also add things like Worcestershire sauce, cheese, pieces of ham, bacon, salami, or corned beef. Cook the eggs over low heat, stirring them with the spatula so they won't stick to the pan. For really fluffy, light eggs, cook them over *very low* heat, and gently push the eggs toward the center of the pan as they cook (this takes practice).

*The Fruit Frappe.* This is a drink you make in a blender with a glass of milk, a sliced banana, and a couple of ice cubes. That's it. Put it in, turn it on, and you've got a creamy, dreamy goodie that even a nutritionist could love.

You can make a frappe with other fruits, such as strawberries or peaches, but then you may have to add some sugar or honey to make it sweet enough for your taste. You can also add a half cup (or less) of yogurt, frozen yogurt, or ice cream, which will add calories; or cinnamon, which won't. By the way, people on a reducing diet make these drinks with low-fat milk, and many people (even skinny ones)

fore you slip the egg into the pan and start frying it. For sunny-side-up eggs, cook them without a lid until the yolk is firm and the white turns really white. For "easy over," you're supposed to flip over the egg with a spatula. But if that's too hard, you can get almost the same effect by covering the pan while they're cooking. When the eggs are done, slide them out of the pan like it better that way. The fruit frappe is also a good in-a-hurry breakfast.

*The English Muffin Pizza.* If you called this creation a "pizza" to someone living in Italy, he'd laugh his head off. Anyway, it's tasty, fast, and nourishing. You make it by cutting a muffin in half, then putting tomato or pizza sauce on both pieces. Use sauce from a jar or can, unless you're lucky enough to have some of the real stuff left over from a spaghetti dinner. Then put a slice of mozzarella cheese (Muenster will do in a pinch) on each muffin half, and sprinkle with grated cheese, oregano, and pepper. Put them on a baking sheet and bake in an oven that's set for about 350° for 10–15 minutes, or until the cheese is bubbly on top.

This is a great after-school snack to make for your friends, and so is our next suggestion:

*The Grilled Tomato (Bacon) and Cheese Sandwich.* Butter two slices of bread. Put one slice aside, and place the other, butter side down, on a plate or piece of plastic wrap. Put a slice of cheese (American, Swiss, Muenster, or mozzarella melts best, but almost any kind will do), a slice or two of tomato, and, if you're ambitious enough to have fried it beforehand, a couple of slices of bacon, on the bread. Put the other slice of bread on top, butter side up. Now you've got the buttered sides on the top and bottom, *not* inside the sand-

wich. Fry the sandwich, first on one side, then on the other, in a frying pan over medium heat. Each side should come out golden brown, and the cheese should be all gooey, and the tomato all soft and warm, and the bacon all crisp, and . . . all this goes great with a cool glass of milk or apple juice. *Any*time.

## Lunches-to-Go: Picking and Packing

If you make your own lunches for school, try to pick foods that make up as balanced a meal as you can, considering the limitations. (It's hard to pack meat, vegetables, salad, and soup in a brown paper bag, or even a lunchbox.) A good compromise lunch-on-the-go could be:

A sandwich (to avoid the soggies, go easy on the mayonnaise or mustard and, sorry, no grilled cheese because it doesn't taste the same cold)

A piece of fruit or raisins or nuts — and/or

A crunchy raw vegetable, such as celery or carrots

Milk (which you can buy at school)

A goodie (candy, cookie, cake, or pie) if you must, but don't skip the fruit or vegetable.

Another good lunchbox food is hard-boiled egg. But you have to remember to do this ahead of time. If you have a Thermos, you can fill it with some hot soup.

Pack the different things in your lunch separately, or they'll end up together (the old mayonnaise-on-the-banana, cookie-crumbs-on-the-bologna syndrome). Use aluminum foil or clear plastic or waxed paper, and don't wrap up the pickles *with* the sandwich unless you like pickled bread. If you have to bring anything in a container, make sure the lid's on tight. Pack things that crush easily, such as potato chips and pretzels, on top.

## Cooking for the Crew

Up to now, this section has been about taking care of your own cooking needs.

But you may want to (or be asked to) really do a number and cook a "real" meal for your whole family. This means: 1) learning to cook the individual dishes in the meal, 2) choosing a balanced menu, 3) getting prepared, 4) figuring out how to get everything done at the same time, and 5) cleaning up as you go.

1. There are two ways to learn to cook a dish: either watch it being made or follow a recipe. Whenever you have a choice, pick

the first way. Watching is worth a hundred thousand words: it makes it all so much easier. Once you know the basics, it's fine (and fun) to use cookbooks. But at first, look and learn, especially from people in your family. Not only will you catch on faster, but you'll be learning to make things your family likes. You can find a recipe for the best Chicken à la Ala in the world, but if your brothers hate chicken — forget it!

2. Choose a menu that's balanced, using a wide variety of foods (see NUTRITION) and *never* having too many foods of the same type. Potatoes and spaghetti and bread and rice and cake is just *too much starch*. The same goes for a meal of meat, eggs, cheese, and chicken. That's almost all protein, and

no roughage (or fiber) — the green and crunchy stuff. The idea is to mix and match. You don't have to hit it perfectly, but you should be on the right track. One way to check out the balance of your meal is to look at the colors: if they're all the same (white potatoes, spaghetti, bread, rice, and

angel food cake), you're not only on the wrong track, you may be up the creek. No fair dyeing the mashed potatoes purple: no one will eat them that way anyhow.

3. Once you know what you want to serve, make sure you've got *all* the ingredients. This takes planning. Sure, you have the ham, but what about the mustard? You have the lettuce, but where is the dressing? Sometimes, you can substitute one ingredient for another, but try to be as well prepared as you can be. That also means setting up the equipment you'll need and knowing how to use each piece.

4. Some people can make individual dishes like a dream, but have nightmares about putting it all together. The problem is timing. Different foods take different amounts of time to cook, and you can mess up a meal (but good!) if you don't take this into consideration. Suppose you were cooking steak, baked potatoes, and canned peas, and you started cooking everything at the same time. The potatoes take an hour, the steak about fifteen minutes, and the peas five minutes. In fifteen minutes, the steak would be ready to eat, the peas would be dry as a bone, and the potatoes would be hard as rocks. Well, you could eat the steak, crunch on the peas, and save the potatoes for des-

sert. . . . This timing business is not easy, which is another reason we urge you to watch a good cook at work as a way of learning to do it yourself.

5. Whenever possible, clean up the mess you make right after you make it. (Got that?) The idea is to do a little at a time, so that you won't have a monumental mess at the end. Wipe up the counter tops often, and fill bowls and pans with water so they'll soak and be easier to wash. If you're waiting for something to finish cooking, *don't just stand there:* wash a bowl or put the sugar back in the cupboard. You'll be glad you did in the end.

# (At Last!) Making Goodies for Fun and Profit

This part of the cooking section is less for survival than for fun. After all, kids do not live by carrot sticks alone. There are some goodies that are too good to be ignored, and we're not going to. Here are our favorite recipes for two biggies of the sweet-tooth world: fudge brownies and home-made lemonade. Not only can you make these things for fun, but you can sell them for a profit (see JOBS — FOR YOU). Just one more small word about nutrition (after all, you *are* a growing person): don't make cookies and other sweets a way of life. We'll say no more — on with the recipes!

## THE OFFICIAL AH-SWEET-MYSTERY-OF-LIFE FUDGE BROWNIES

INGREDIENTS:
> *2 squares of unsweetened chocolate*
> *½ cup butter*
> *1 cup sugar*
> *2 eggs*
> *½ cup sifted all-purpose flour*
> *⅛ teaspoon baking powder*
> *½ teaspoon vanilla*
> *½ cup chopped walnuts (if you want to go nuts)*

GET READY: Preheat the oven to 325°. And prepare an 8- or 9-inch square pan by rubbing butter or shortening on the inside bottom and sides.

GET SET: Beat the eggs in a small bowl and set them aside. Melt the chocolate and butter in the top of a double boiler, or over a *very low* flame, being very careful not to burn it.

When this is melted, take the pot from the heat and beat the sugar, eggs, and vanilla into the melted chocolate. Mix the flour and baking powder together. Then fold this into the chocolate mixture.

("Fold" just means mixing by using two movements: going down through the mixture, and turning it over by scraping the spoon across the bottom of the bowl.) And that's it. Unless you want to add the nuts. In which case, add the nuts — you mad, impetuous cook.

BAKE! Pour the mixture into the pan and bake for 30 minutes. Don't overcook if you want them to be good and fudgie.

even some wintry afternoon by the fire), here's how you do it.

INGREDIENTS:
- *6 cups of water*
- *1 cup sugar*
- *½ cup lemon juice (about four medium lemons)*
- *½ teaspoon salt*
- *A fairly large pot (no, not your Uncle Albert's stomach)*
- *A large pitcher (no, not the guy on your softball team)*

COOL IT! Be patient: we know they smell sweet and irresistible. Better wait till they cool, though, then cut them into squares, and, finally, eat!

## THE OFFICIAL HONEST-TO-GOODNESS MADE-FROM-SCRATCH REAL LEMONADE

Why would anyone want to make lemonade from scratch, when you can buy frozen lemonade or powdered mixes? Why? Because it's better, that's why. And if you have the time some warm summer day (or

MIX IT UP: Put the water, sugar, and salt into the pot and stir it up. Boil for 2 minutes. Pour this slightly gloppy syrup into a large pitcher and chill it for at least 1 hour. Meanwhile, squeeze the lemons. When the syrup is chilled, add the lemon juice to it, and — that's it! Pour it over ice and serve in a tall glass.

*Note to lemonade lovers:* Experiment to see how sweet or tart you like it by adding more or less sugar. You can also add a sprig of fresh mint, a cherry, or a strawberry when you serve it. That's class.

# CUTS AND SCRAPES

## Clean Cuts

When you get a cut, even a little one, you may not like the look of all that blood. But the blood is actually helping to clean out the wound and starting to heal it.

Of course, you don't want it to bleed too much. If you have read the section on BLEEDING, for serious wounds, you know about direct pressure: holding a clean cloth against the wound and pressing on it. Do this for a few minutes, and don't keep lifting the cloth up to look at the cut (it won't go away). When the bleeding stops, wash the cut with warm water and soap. Then put on a bandage.

If the cut turns out to be more serious than you first thought, keep up the direct pressure and get to a doctor.

## Clean Scrapes, Too

Since you've probably had your share of skinned knees and scraped elbows, we don't have to tell you what a scrape is like. As you know, a scrape hurts, but it doesn't bleed much. That means that pieces of dirt or stone can stick in there. So you have to wash a scrape *very* carefully with warm water and soap to get everything out. Sometimes you even have to scrub the spot with a stiff brush. We know. This hurts even more. But it's better than getting an infection.

By the way, scrapes are sometimes called *abrasions*. Don't be confused by the big word — it's the same old everyday scrape.

## What Not to Do

• DON'T lick your wound or put your mouth over a scrape or cut, or breathe on it. You could be spreading germs into an open wound.
• DON'T let anything that isn't clean — including your own dirty fingers or your old used tissue — touch your wound.
• DON'T bandage a cut until it's cleaned out.

See also FIRST AID.

◆ NOTES:

 *Through*

## ❧ DELIVERIES ❧

Say you're expecting a delivery — your mom or dad told you that someone would be bringing a package from Macy's or Lacy's or Dave's Drip-Dry Cleaners. When the doorbell rings, *do not open the door right away.* Instead, look through a window or peephole on the door (if there is one) and ask the delivery person to identify himself. Never say, "Are you the man from Lacy's who was supposed to come at four o'clock?" Then, all the person has to say is yes, and you'll have no way of knowing whether it's the truth. But if the information the person gives you is the same as the information your parent gave you, and you think the caller is what he or she claims to be, open the door and accept the delivery.

If you're *not* expecting a delivery, or a caller says he has to read the gas meter, or make a repair, or give you a message, or whatever, *do not open the door at all* and call a parent or a neighbor. If you strongly suspect this person is up to no good, call the police immediately.

Important: also check out SAFETY AND SECURITY.

▶ NOTES:

_____
_____
_____
_____
_____

## ❧ DIETING ❧

There's only one good reason for going on a reducing diet: you're too fat. *Don't* go on a diet because your best friend is on one, or

because you want to look like that new teenage model, or because one pair of jeans doesn't fit. (Hey! They may have

shrunk. See LAUNDRY.) Dieting is a weighty matter, no kidding. To lose pounds, you have to eat less food, and if you're not careful you might not get the nourishment you need. Even if you don't want to grow wider, you do want to grow up.

Guess what? There's also only one good reason for going on a weight-gaining diet: you're too thin. Some people think that if they don't look like Ms. or Mr. Cosmic Universal World, they're too skinny and must immediately put on weight — in all the right places.

Take a good, honest look at yourself. If you're really too fat or too thin — bearing in mind that nobody is perfect — then read this section. If you have any doubts, talk it over with a parent or even your doctor. Set goals for yourself: "I want to get in shape by summer," "I want to lose weight by Christmas." Make sure your goals are reasonable and that you're giving yourself enough time.

## Take It Off

Okay, you really are too heavy. What should you do? The answer is simple, but doing it can be hard. You simply have to eat less, especially sweet, fatty, and starchy foods. It sometimes seems impossible (IMPOSSIBLE!) to give up goodies like cookies and potato chips and choco-

late. Even talking about these foods makes your mouth water. But, let's face it, that's probably how you became overweight in the first place. If you really want to be thinner, you'll have to grit your teeth and close your mouth — especially when you're around food.

That's the bad news. The good news is a diet doesn't have to be that strict. Sure, there are some that tell you exactly what to eat and when to eat it. They give instructions like: *Lunch:* 2 ounces of chicken, 1 shredded leaf of lettuce, ½ piece of whole-grain toast with ¼ teaspoon of margarine, 4 ounces of tomato juice. How can you stick to a diet like that? You'd have to go around with a scale, a set of measuring spoons and cups, a lettuce shredder, and a head full of instructions.

*The Official Kids' Survival Kit* recommends a simple system of adding and subtracting (no multiplication or division . . . we promise!). You *add* things that are nourishing and not fattening, you *subtract* things that are likely to put on pounds. Here are the seven steps:

## THE OFFICIAL SEVEN SUGGESTIONS FOR WEIGHT LOSS

1. Eat two or three crunchy, juicy fruits and vegetables every day — things like apples, oranges, carrots. Having these kinds of goodies to munch on will make it easier to give up some of the things you shouldn't have.

2. Go easy on bread and butter, say "No, thank you" to desserts (except for fruit), and cut down on fatty or fried foods and starchy foods like potatoes, pasta (spaghetti, macaroni), and rice.

3. Drink water or sparkling water instead of cola and other sweet drinks. If you must, drink sugar-free soft drinks, but don't overdo it. They won't make you fat, but they're not that great for you, either.

4. Try to give up fattening snacks. If you absolutely, positively must have something to nibble on, eat a small piece of fruit or some raw vegetables — things that aren't loaded with calories.

*And Now, a Word about Calories:* You've probably heard about the little devils, haven't you? They provide energy, and your body burns off calories every day. But if you take in more calories than you need, the extra ones get stored — as fat. When you diet, you take in fewer calories than your body uses, so the stored fat is burned off.

Some foods are high in calories, some are low. (If you want to find out how many calories certain foods have, check a calorie counter.) But the important thing in dieting is to avoid the *really* high-calorie foods that are also low in nutrition. These are the true baddies of the dieting world: cola, ice cream, cake, pie, cookies, french fries, chocolate (sorry about that). Notice that most of these baddies are sweet. That brings us to the next step:

5. Don't touch that sugar bowl! Cut back *drastically* on sugar and all sweet foods. If you do nothing else, this alone will help you lose weight.

6. Don't have second or third helpings of anything that isn't super low-calorie. One potato isn't too bad; four are bad news.

7. Red meats (like beef and pork) are more fattening than light meats (like veal). Poultry, especially chicken, is good for diets — if it's not fried — because it's lower in calories than most meats and is high in protein. The same is true for fish. We know you don't usually get a choice at home, but it's good

to know about all this. That way, you'll make the right choices when you get the chance. And you'll be warned about eating too much beef or pork (cut all the fat off) when it's served to you.

## TO TELL OR NOT TO TELL

First of all, always tell your parents about your diet. They can help by serving smaller portions at dinner, by not offering you seconds, by fixing low-calorie meals, by not filling the cupboard with fattening snacks. They may even join you on your diet, which would make mealtimes easier for everyone. (But don't count on it — never try to force anyone into going on a diet; you've got enough to do taking care of yourself.)

Your parents may want you to see a doctor, especially if you have to lose a lot of weight. If so, follow the doctor's instructions as best you can. And be honest. If you simply can't stick to the diet you're given, say so. Together, you can work out a diet that really works — for you.

So whom *shouldn't* you tell? Many people will tease you when they know you're on a diet. Some even try to tempt you to go off it. And who needs that? Some of these people don't mean to be mean. They may think you look really adorable with all that baby fat, or may be sincerely worried that you'll get sick if you lose weight. Others are jealous: there's nothing more they'd like to do than lose some weight themselves. They can't do it, and they don't want you to do it either. Well, that's their problem. The best way to avoid teasing or tempting is not to mention your diet to too many people. No one will notice what you're eating unless you talk about it. By the time these troublesome people notice that you've lost weight, it will be too late for them to cause you any grief.

*EXERCISE*
Here's an old joke for you: What's the best exercise for a dieter? Answer: pushing yourself away from the table. (We said it was *old,* not *funny.*) Besides that little

trick, you might try a routine of regular exercises. It tones you up and makes you look and feel thinner. Who knows, it could even help you stick to your diet. (See EXERCISE.)

*KEEPING IT OFF*
Once you're as thin as you should be, keep the weight from coming back by sticking to your diet and adding — a little at a time — some of the things you gave up. When you're the right weight, you can have that plate of coconut-almond-mocha-custard pudding. Just don't overdo it . . . or do it too often.

## Putting It On

When most people hear the word "diet," they think it means losing weight. And it usually does. That's because more people are now overweight than underweight, so the phrase "reducing diet" has been shortened to just plain "diet." But diet really means *what* you eat: it can be planned to make you lose weight, stay the same, or gain weight.

### 110  120  **130**  140

It's usually better to be on the thin side (especially as an adult), but there is such a thing as too thin. The danger here is that you'll be a little weak, and if you should get ill and lose even more weight, you could be in trouble.

Well, if you have to eat less to lose weight, then you have to eat more to gain weight. Right. And if you have to give up sweets to lose weight, then you should load up on sugar-rich foods to gain weight. WRONG! No matter what your weight is — even if it's perfect — you always have to eat a well-balanced diet (more about that under NUTRITION). We know you've heard that before, but there's a good reason: it's true. If you're underweight and stuff yourself with candy bars and soda, you could get sick and end up losing even more weight.

But look on the bright side. You can have some of the no-nos that your chubbier friends can't have: milk shakes and malteds, breads and rolls, pizza! And you can have second, third, even fourth helpings of meat, vegetables, pasta, fruits, and other good things.

If you eat like a horse and still don't gain weight, you may need a physical checkup. Don't worry. Everyone's body works differently. Yours just may burn up calories more quickly. Talk to your parents about it.

## Fads and Facts

Fads come and go, and thank goodness they go. Check out these fad diets.

1. *The Banana Diet.* Nothing but bananas for a whole week. You either lost weight or turned yellow (or both).

2. *The Grapefruit Diet.* This time you not only turned yellow, you ended up with a permanent pucker.

3. *The All-Ice-Cream Diet.* Sound delicious? First listen. The idea was that you'd get so sick of ice cream after a while that you couldn't eat another lick, so you wouldn't be eating anything and you'd lose weight. Really healthy, right?

Even if diets like these "work," that is, you lose weight, they don't work for long. As soon as you get off them, you go back to your old eating habits and quickly (too quickly), the pounds come back again. Stay away from this kind of diet madness!

## Reward Offered

Rewards help give you the willpower to stay on your diet. So promise yourself something special when you've lost (or gained) a certain number of pounds, or when you've stayed on your diet a certain number of days. Your reward can be anything (except fattening foods): a new record album, a game, or just getting to wear all those jeans that don't fit now.

## ❧ DISHES ❧

### The Step-by-Step Sink

Easy! If you've only got one or two, just wipe them clean with a warm soapy sponge, then rinse well. If there's a whole sinkful, follow these steps:

1. Wipe off and throw away all scraps of food from each dish.
2. Close the drain in the sink and pile in the dirty dishes — *carefully,* so they won't break.
3. Add a little dishwashing liquid and enough very warm or hot water (don't burn yourself!) to just about cover the dishes.
4. Wipe each dish with a sponge, washcloth, or soap pad.
5. Let the soapy, dirty water drain out of the sink.
6. Refill the sink with clean clear water and rinse the dishes well.

If you're using an automatic dishwasher, read the section on DISHWASHERS.

### Pots and Pans Can Be a Pain

If you have some that are hard to clean, soak them in very hot, soapy water. Do this first, before you start on the rest of the dishes, and let the pots and pans soak up the suds until you've got all the others done. Then use a scrubbing pad, and, well — *scrub!*

### The Sooner the Better

The longer dirty dishes stay dirty, the harder they are to wash. Some foods, like oatmeal, eggs, or spaghetti sauce, get so

## Dry Time

You can either:

1. Stack the just-washed-and-rinsed dishes on a dish rack and let them drip-dry, then put them away later. Or,

2. Towel-dry each dish with a clean cloth and put them away as you dry them.

Either way, handle dishes carefully. Otherwise, you might have to turn to the section on BROKEN DISHES/GLASS.

hard after a while that they stick to the plates like cement. This is no fun to clean. Also, remember that if it's your job to do the dishes, and you put it off and put it off, you're going to make the rest of the family annoyed: no one likes to go to the sink for a glass of water and have to fight through a pile of greasy pots and pans. So, you'll end up both doing the work (sooner or later) and having people angry with you.

◗ NOTES:

_____
_____
_____
_____
_____

## ෨ DISHWASHERS ෨

Since all dishwashers are not exactly the same, you'll have to find out how yours works. But here are a few things you should know about using any brand of dishwasher:

• Always scrape and rinse the dishes (especially the pots and pans) before you put them in the machine.

• Load the machine correctly: this usually means putting the plates and other big stuff on the bottom rack, the cups, glasses, and other small stuff on the top, and the knives, forks, and spoons in the special holder.

• Don't waste water by running the machine with only a few things in it.

• *Always* use a detergent made especially for dishwashers. *Never* use any other kind of liquid or powder. Why? Because it won't do the job, for one thing. And for another, the machine could clog and overflow, making you the star of that great new horror film, "The Soapsuds That Ate Your Kitchen."

• Don't take the dishes out as soon as the machine stops. Wait awhile for them to cool down.

See also APPLIANCES.

♦ NOTES:

## ❧ DOCTOR/DENTIST VISITS ❧

### What's Up, Doc?

Most of the time, you're seeing a doctor for a routine checkup. It's usually for school or camp, or just a regular yearly visit. There's certainly nothing to be afraid of — the doctor will be doing things like listening to your chest with a stethoscope, and asking you to open wide and say "Aaahh!"

But some people get weak in the knees just thinking about blood tests or injections, even though neither of these things hurts more than getting your finger pricked. If you're like this, *tell the doctor about it.* Then, he or she will usually ask you to lie down when tests are being done, and this will make you feel better.

You're not alone if you're the squea-

mish type, and no one will think it's strange. Of course, you're not going to start carrying on like a maniac and making everyone in the doctor's office wish they worked for a veterinarian. You're just

⚕ ⚕ ⚕ ⚕ ⚕

calmly and honestly going to tell what you're feeling: "I get really jumpy when they do a blood test." Or, "Once, when I got a shot, I fainted." Or, "I'm scared." Period.

Even if you're not a bit jittery, you may wonder about what's going on. *Ask questions about anything you don't understand.* You should know:

- What is being done
- Why it's being done
- What the results are

Let's say the doctor begins to take your blood pressure and puts this band around your arm and starts pumping up a kind of bulb. You should be told that your blood pressure is being taken. Fine. So what *is* your blood pressure? *Ask.* And don't take "normal" for an answer: ask for the numbers. Why? Because you want to know as much about yourself as you can. Suppose your blood pressure is a little on the low side. If you know that, and you know what your "okay" range is, then you won't be upset if you're told that your reading is low at another time. Or suppose your "normal" temperature is *not* 98.6. It could be a little higher or lower, and still be "normal" — for *you.* Knowing the facts is important.

Sometimes, doctors mumble things like "Hmmm" when they're checking your heart or lungs or knees or whatever. Ask what that hmmm means. After all, it's *your* heart, lungs, knees, or whatever.

If you're seeing a doctor for something special, like a broken bone or an allergy that's acting up, you may have some specific questions. "Why does my arm itch so much in this cast?" "Last week, I hit my hand on my desk. Does that mean the bone won't heal now?" "If I'm allergic to

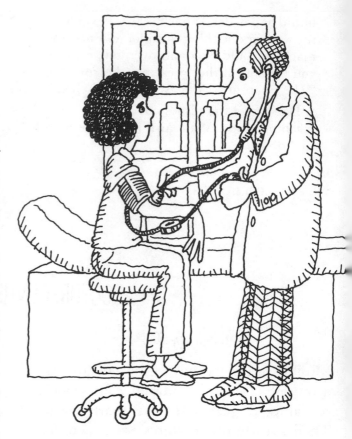

dogs, am I allergic to horses, too?" You can write down your questions, or just think about what you want to ask. But remember, the doctor is not a mind reader. If you don't ask the questions, you won't get the answers.

As much as possible, you should understand the results of the doctor's tests. (Sometimes, this means waiting for a laboratory report.) We say "as much as possible" because it isn't always easy (or necessary) for doctors to explain every single thing to their patients. The point is that it shouldn't be a big mystery. A doctor's visit should not give you things to worry about or wonder about.

## Dentists Are Doctors, Too

Much of what we said about doctor's visits is the same for dental appointments. The

important thing is to *ask questions* and to *be honest.*

Find out:

• What — if anything — is wrong with your teeth
• What needs to be done
• How long it will take
• How many visits you will need
• If it will hurt
• If you will get an injection or gas to ease the pain
• How this will make you feel

Most people are a little nervous about these visits, at least until they get to know the dentist. And trying to be a superhero makes it worse. Dentists talk about the "white-knuckle" types: people who say they're just fine, but clutch the edges of the chair so hard that their knuckles turn white. On the other hand, many people find that just admitting they're a little scared helps a lot. And it usually doesn't turn out to be as bad as you imagined.

## Dryers

See LAUNDRY.

## Dusting

See CLEANING HOUSE.

When it comes to electrical repairs, there are three basic rules:

*Rule 1.* Big problems should be handled by an expert.

*Rule 2.* Treat electricity with great respect.

*Rule 3.* Don't mess with it *at all* if any part of you is wet: hands, clothing, shoes — *anything.*

## Let There Be Light

Not all electrical problems are big ones, and there are some repairs you can do easily. For instance, you can certainly change a light bulb. You say you've never done it? Here's how:

1. Turn off the electricity by flicking the switch off, and, to be extra-cautious (see *Rule 2,* above), unplug the lamp.

2. Wait until the bulb is cool enough to handle. (Hot bulbs are easily dropped and can shatter.) Then unscrew it from the socket.

3. Check to see how many "watts" the old bulb is (it's clearly printed on top of the bulb) and get a new bulb that's the same or close to it.

4. Screw the new bulb in. When it feels snug, plug in the lamp and turn the switch on. If it doesn't work immediately, it may

not be screwed in tightly enough (check it), or there may be a short circuit in the lamp. If so, forget it: use another lamp and tell your parents about it.

## Blowing Your Fuse (or Circuit Breaker)

Fuses and circuit breakers are fantastic safety devices: they protect the electrical system in your home or apartment. If you're using too much electricity at once, or if an appliance is defective, a fire could start. Instead of that happening, a fuse will "blow" or a circuit breaker will "trip," and the electricity will automatically be cut off in part of the house (the part where the problem is).

Most homes have several fuses and circuit breakers, each one controlling a different room or part of the house. They are located in a box (see illustration) which is usually in the basement or somewhere in your apartment. Have your parent show you where the box is and explain to you which fuses or circuit breakers control which outlets or rooms, if the box isn't clearly labeled.

### *WHEN A FUSE BLOWS*
Changing a fuse means removing the old one and replacing it with a new one, so

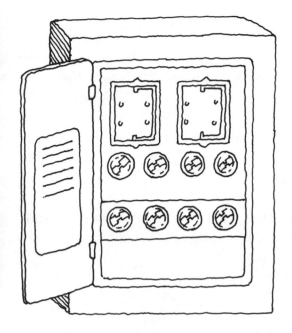

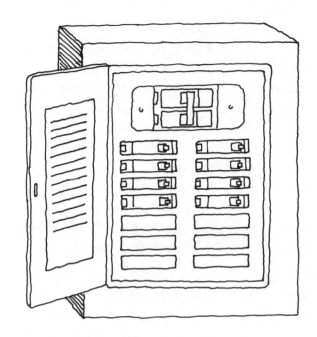

find out in advance where the new fuses are kept. To change a fuse, do this:

1. Turn off the switches for all appliances and lights in the room where the electricity has gone off.

2. Go to the fuse box and locate the blown fuse. It's easy to spot: most often, the metal strip behind the little window will be melted, or the little window will be slightly discolored (see illustration).

3. With dry hands, unscrew the fuse just as you would a light bulb. If you have a fuse puller, use it.

4. Fuses are color-coded and labeled so you can tell their "ampere" rating (15A, 25A, etc.). Replace the old fuse by screwing in a new one of the same rating.

## WHEN A CIRCUIT BREAKER TRIPS

In newer homes, circuit-breaker boxes are more common than fuse boxes. They serve the same purpose (safety) as fuses, but they don't have to be replaced. If a circuit breaker trips, do this:

1. Turn off all the switches for all appliances and lights in the room where the electricity went out.

2. Go to the circuit-breaker box and look at the circuit-breaker switch that controls that part of the house.

3. If the switch is on the "off" position, switch it to "on." If the switch is already on "on," switch it to "off," then to "on" again. Sometimes, you have to switch it back and forth a few times.

### IT DID IT AGAIN!

After you have changed the fuse or switched on the circuit breaker, return to the room where the electricity went out and switch on only the lights and appliances you really need. (Avoid putting on the air conditioner *and* the toaster *and* the hair dryer *and* the stereo *and* . . .) If the electricity goes off again, it would be best to use another room and make the best of it until your parents get home. The problem may need professional attention.

### LET YOUR PARENTS SEE THE LIGHT

Whenever you change a fuse or use a circuit breaker, let your parents know what you've done. You could even mention changing light bulbs because they'll want to get new bulbs to have a supply on hand.

## Lights Off — Everywhere

If the electricity goes off in the whole house, it probably isn't a blown fuse or a tripped circuit breaker. Check the neighbors' houses or apartments: there may be outside trouble affecting the whole neighborhood. If that's the case, see BLACKOUTS.

See also APPLIANCES and ELECTRICAL SHOCK, if you have to.

❯ NOTES:

_____

_____

_____

_____

  ## ELECTRICAL SHOCK

Many people don't realize how powerful shocks from certain appliances can be, and are very careless when handling them. Usually, a shock is pretty mild, and just gives the person a bit of a jolt. But occasionally it's much worse, and the person must be rescued.

Remember that the electrical power is still running through the equipment — *and through the person.* Act fast, but don't touch anything until you've disconnected the appliance from its outlet. And don't even do this unless your hands and clothing are dry, and you're standing in a dry place.

If you have to separate the person from

the appliance, use something dry *with no metal on it,* like a wooden broomstick or a piece of rope or cloth.

After the person is away from the source of danger, treat for SHOCK, and BURNS, if there are any, and get help!

anything but dry wood or fabric — especially not with anything made of metal. And don't do a thing if you're wet.

See also FIRST AID, and APPLIANCES for tips on preventing electrical shock.

## Don't Be Shocked Yourself

Again: don't ever touch the victim or the appliance until the current is turned off or the person is separated from the source of the shock. Never touch the person with

▶ NOTES:

_____

_____

_____

_____

## ❧ ELEVATORS ❧

It doesn't happen often, but elevators have been known to break down or get stuck in between floors. If this occurs, press the "alarm" button, and wait as patiently as you can. Make some noise if it makes you feel better, but try not to get too upset because you *will* be rescued eventually (no one has ever been permanently "lost" on an elevator). Sooner or later, someone will

hear you — or will want to use the elevator — and a repairman will be on the job.

Other things you should know about elevators are: don't use them if there's a fire (use the stairs instead), and don't get on an elevator with anyone you feel uneasy about (see also the section on SAFETY AND SECURITY).

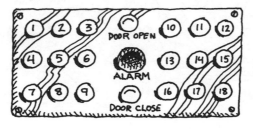

 **✎ EMERGENCIES ✎**

## What They Are and What They Aren't

An emergency IS:

• A dangerous situation — such as a fire, flood, or gas leak

• A serious accident — such as a broken bone or heavy bleeding

• A life-threatening illness — such as an asthma attack or allergic reaction

An emergency ISN'T:

• Losing your homework assignment

• Spilling spaghetti on your clown costume just before the play

• Not having one ingredient for the coconut cookies you're baking

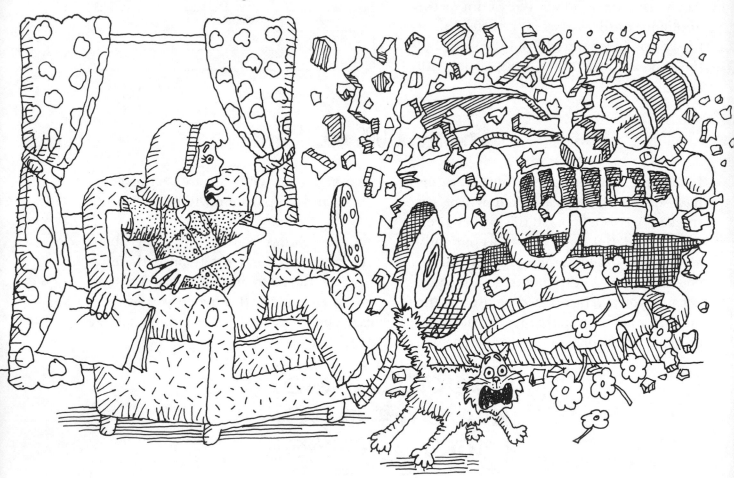

These things may be important to you — but they're *not* emergencies. And it's a very bad idea to act as if they were. Every time you set up a cry of "Emergency!" you make people very, very concerned. That's fine when it's a real emergency: the people you alert will be grateful. But when it's not, they will be angry.

## UNREAL EMERGENCIES: TWO SENSELESS SCENES

*Scene One:* Your mother is in the middle of an important meeting at work when she gets a frantic call from you. She's upset, she drops everything (including her hot cup of coffee on her boss's lap), and runs to the phone. You tell her that your hamster, Alexandra, has escaped. *Uh-oh . . .*

*Scene Two:* You're in the middle of a great soccer game. Your coach comes running over to say that your father is on the phone and it's an emergency. Even though you're afraid your team might lose without you, you rush across the field and up the stairs and down the hall, and, finally, you get to the phone. Your father says he's run out of shaving cream and could you pick some up on the way home from school. *Moan . . .*

## A REAL EMERGENCY

Okay. You've got a real, genuine, actual, honest-to-Pete emergency on your hands. This is the time to be very aggressive. Try to reach the right people — immediately! — and don't be embarrassed about interrupting *anyone,* at any time of the day or night. Stay as calm as you can, but make it clear how important it is to get help.

Remember this, too: when it comes to emergencies, age is no object. If you're the one who knows what to do — even if you're the youngest person there — you're the one who can do the most good. That's why it's a good idea to read over the sections on different kinds of emergencies so that you'll be prepared to act if a real one comes up.

See also FIRE, FIRST AID, GAS FUMES, etc., and "Emergency Calls," under PHONE CALLS.

▶ NOTES:

_____

_____

_____

_____

When you find yourself alone with children you're in charge of — at a babysitting job or at home with younger brothers and sisters — you might have to think of ways to keep them entertained. And out of trouble. You don't have to put together a nightclub act with a cast of thousands (or two, even), but you should have a few tricks up your sleeve.

## The One-to-Three Crew

With kids this age, it's best to play with their own games and toys. They like things like stuffed animals, pull toys, and blocks, and have their own special ways of using them. Play along with them. Then, you can show them new ways to use their things, making up games and stories — maybe some that you liked when you were little.

You can also read stories from their own books. No matter how many times they've

heard them before, they'll want to hear them again — especially when a new person reads them. Don't be surprised if they know some of the words by heart. That doesn't mean they're bored, but that they

really love those words. Encourage them to "read" along. And if there are pictures, ask about them: "Who is that?" "What is he doing?" You can also make it more exciting by reading with feeling. Make your voice different for each of the characters. It's goofy, but fun, and guaranteed to please. You can also bring along your own books, tell them old favorites from memory, or make up your own stories.

## The Three-to-Six Set

Again, almost anyone, of any age, loves a good story. The "older" kids in this group can also read to you, which gives them a chance to show off, and you a chance to rest your voice.

Use the child's own toys and games whenever possible. Make jigsaw puzzles together, play checkers, or TV computer games. But if these things are not around, or if the child is bored with them, have a few no-equipment-needed games in mind to play anytime: old favorites, such as Simon Says, Blind Man's Bluff, Hide-and-Seek.

Anything to do with pretending is fun for children of this age. A box becomes a boat; a broom, a flag; a paper-towel roll, a telescope. Use what's around, and let the children do as much of the creative "work" as possible. If, for example, you set the child off on one sort of pretend adventure (a boat trip, via milk carton, to the North Pole), and the child suddenly takes off on another (he's an Indian, canoeing over the rapids), go with it.

Let them be creative with paper: cutting it up (carefully), folding it, and, of course, drawing on it. If they run out of ideas on what to draw, give them some. Ask them to draw their favorite animal, a happy dream they've had, the way they think they look. For a good laugh, ask them to draw the way they think *you* look. (You may be in for a shock.) It's best not to get into scary things, like drawing monsters or wild beasts, when you're alone with children, especially before bedtime. (Bad dreams.)

If crafts are your bag, help them make things with pipe cleaners, dough, clay, even uncooked macaroni. Just don't pick a project that is too long (they'll get bored), too complicated (they'll get frustrated), or too messy (*you'll* have to clean up).

This is also the perfect opportunity to do those magic tricks you've been practicing, or to play songs on your guitar or harmonica. You get to try your skills out on a live audience, and they get to be en-

tertained. Try to include them in some active way: singing along, choosing the songs, picking a card, or being your assistant.

## Six and Up

When you're in charge of children closer to your own age, the best course of action is to let them choose the activities. (Within reason, of course.) You can also teach

them games you like: anything from that old favorite, Tic-Tac-Toe, to word games, such as "Stinky Pinky," which, by some strange coincidence, is explained right here.

*Rules:* You give a clue (definition) and the other person has to think of two rhyming words that fit the meaning. Such as:

Q: An overweight rodent? — A: Fat Rat

Q: A tired flower? — A: Lazy Daisy

Q: A smiling father? — A: Glad Dad (or, Happy Pappy!)

Or how about this one: What do you call a person who's watching children and is angry because things are not going well? *Answer:* A Bitter Sitter.

For young babies, see INFANTS.

# Etiquette

See MANNERS.

# EXERCISE

## Don't Just Sit There!

If you're one of those kids who's a sports fanatic, or if you get straight A+'s in gym, or take dance class, or walk two miles a day to school (and two miles back), or if you're just plain active all day, you're probably getting all the exercise you need. And that's great.

But if you lead a low-energy, lackadaisical life — if you spend most of the time sitting around and are driven wherever you go — you should definitely consider putting more energy into your life with an exercise program.

## What Exercise Won't Do

Sorry, but no amount of exercise will change your basic body structure: it can't transform you from short to tall, or vice versa. It can't perform miracles.

## What Exercise Will Do

What it will do is make the most of what you've got. Regular exercise can mean the difference between a strong, trim body (great for your looks and confidence), and a weak, flabby one (great for making you feel like a bag of cement). Exercise can do this for you:

- Put you into better physical condition (by improving the way your heart, lungs, and circulation work)
- Make you stronger
- Help control your weight (by burning up calories that would turn to fat) and redistribute some of it (so it isn't all in your stomach and hips)
- Get rid of flab and make you firmer (all *right!*)
- Help you feel more relaxed
- Help you sleep more soundly (and wake up more refreshed)
- Give you more energy and endurance (you'll be one of those kids in your gym class who never seems to huff, puff, or just lie there, panting)

## How Much Exercise?

"How much" isn't nearly as important as "how often." If you're planning to do ten sit-ups occasionally, don't bother, because nothing will happen. What's needed is a *regular* routine, which means every day, if possible, or at least several times a week. And even though exercise can do great things for you, it won't happen overnight. It takes at least a couple of weeks of regular exercise before you can feel — and see — the results. Set goals for yourself, but give yourself enough time to reach them. Remember, The Hulk wasn't built in a day.

## What Kind of Exercise?

This depends entirely on you. Some people enjoy doing twenty-five Jumping Jacks every morning and night. Others prefer to run a mile each afternoon. Still others like to get their workout on a football field or in a ballet class. Do whatever makes you happy, just as long as you do it. Exercise shouldn't be torture, it should be fun! Here are some suggestions:

*Sports.* If you enjoy a certain sport, why not do it on a regular basis? If you like to swim in the summer, do it a few times a week — all year long. Take advantage of your school's swimming pool, if there is one, or sign up at a local "Y" or youth center with a pool. Or try out for the school basketball team. If you "sort of" like sports, but think you're not athletic, give it a chance before you dismiss the idea altogether. Try out a few different sports until you find one you like — there are so many to choose from: tennis, volleyball, soccer, softball, football, lacrosse, bicycle racing . . . you name it. You say you don't like "competitive" or team sports? Then try one of these: pleasure biking, hiking, horseback riding, skiing — there's even mountain climbing (if you have a friendly, neighborhood mountain)!

*Dance or Gymnastics.* If you've ever watched professional dancers or Olympic gymnasts, you know how graceful their bodies are. Both sports are great ways to get exercise, and kids who are into them really enjoy them. You can join a dance class (ballet, tap, modern, jazz, disco) or a gymnastics class, and if you can only go once a week, practice at home in front of a mirror.

If dance classes are unavailable or inconvenient, or if you think you're a lousy dancer and won't do it in public, do it in private. Put on a tape or record of the

liveliest music you have, and dance — energetically — for a half hour each night. Shake, whirl, bend, and jump to the beat.

*Running, Jogging, and Jumping.* These activities have many pluses: you can do them alone, you don't need fancy equipment, and you can do them whenever you like. Even if there's a hurricane outside, you can always run in place in your basement. Before starting, do a few warm-up exercises, and be sure your shoes are the right ones — it will be easier on your feet.

Jumping rope — even five minutes a day — is also a great form of exercise, as many professional athletes know.

## KEEP MOVING

Even if none of the above turns you on, you can still get some exercise if you just keep moving. For example, don't take the bus, train, or a ride when you have to go a mile or two — WALK. And walk briskly, swinging your arms, taking large steps, and breathing deeply. If you live in an apartment building, use the stairs instead of taking the elevator all the time. You can even exercise when you're lying down in bed by s-t-r-e-t-c-h-i-n-g every part of your body. Make an effort to be aware of your body. Just using it a lot throughout the day can, in itself, be exercise.

## EXERCISE WITH EXERCISES

If you like the idea of a regular exercise program (push-ups, knee bends, and all that), or if you think that it's the only way you're going to get enough exercise, ask your gym teacher to help you work out a program that suits your special needs (perhaps a few exercises that concentrate on areas of your body that need building up — or trimming down). Or, check out your local library where you'll find many excellent books on the subject.

## Exercise and Your Health

If you're in good shape physically, exercise can only improve your good health. But if you've recently been ill or injured, or if you have any special or chronic physical condition, or if you're on a strict reducing diet, be sure to get your doctor's okay before you start any new activity.

 ❧ EYE INJURIES ❧

### "I've Got Something in My Eye"

This is the most common eye injury of all. And it's usually more annoying than serious. It's natural to want to rub your eyes when this happens, but that's the worst thing to do. Remove the speck of dirt or dust as soon as possible by following these steps:

1. Close your eyes for a few minutes. Tears may wash the particle out of the eye and do the work for you.

2. If that doesn't work, gently pull down the lower eyelid so you can see the red lining. If the speck is there, get it out with the corner of a *clean* handkerchief or tissue.

3. If the speck isn't there, gently grasp the lashes of the upper lid between your thumb and forefinger. Draw the upper lid *out and down over the lower lid.* Then tears will probably flush the speck out.

4. If none of this works, flush out the eye with clean warm water. Hold your head over a sink. Pour water into the inner corner of the eye (near the nose) and allow it to run over the eyeball and under the lids. Use at least a quart of water.

If someone you're taking care of gets something in his/her eye, and step 1 doesn't work, follow steps 2, 3, and 4.

DON'T try to remove anything from the eyes with your finger, or (*yipes!*) a toothpick!

DON'T use fluffy material, like cotton balls or swabs or lamb's wool: you could end up with more specks in the eye.

DON'T use any liquid other than warm water to flush out the eyes.

### Something Else

When the "something" in the eye is more than just dust or dirt (like a speck of metal or glass), or if you suspect the speck is really stuck in there, get medical help *at once!* Don't even try to remove the particle. Don't do anything, unless a doctor tells you to. Just make sure you don't rub your eye, and try to keep as still as possible until you get to a doctor or hospital.

# Eye Burns

Eye burns can be caused by drain cleaners, strong laundry and dishwashing detergents, and other cleaning things. Even though you see these things around the house all the time, they can be very dangerous if they get into the eyes. *So act fast.* Don't be fooled if the burning isn't too great at first. It can get worse, and it can even lead to blindness. Here's what to do:

**1. Immediately flood the eye(s) and face with warm water for about ten minutes, *without stopping.*** Lie down or lean over a sink with your head to the side. Hold the lid open and pour water from the inner corner of the eye to the outer corner. Repeat for the other eye if it's also injured.

**2. Call for help!**

**3. Cover the eye(s) loosely with a dry pad or a clean cloth until help arrives, and do not rub the injured eye(s).**

See also FIRST AID.

◆ NOTES:

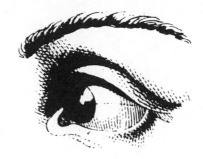

*Just*

# ✒ FAMILY CRISES ✒

By "family crisis," we mean a major problem rather than the day-to-day or emergency situations this book deals with. Such a crisis might be the separation or divorce of your parents; the death of a family member; a serious financial problem, where one or both of your parents lose a job; serious health problems, where someone has to go to the hospital or mental institution for a long period of time; or a problem with the law, where someone has to go on trial or to prison. Even something like moving to a new location can be a crisis in some families.

Major problems such as these can't be covered in a few words, a few pages, maybe not even in a few books. But we can say this: when a family crisis arises, always talk out your feelings with someone: another family member, a friend's parent, a counselor, teacher, or religious leader you feel close to, or an older friend. You'll also find that these kinds of situations lead to some lesser problems, which you can deal with more easily than the crisis itself.

We hope you find some help in the sections on ANGER, and LONELINESS.

# ✒ FEARS ✒

## No Fear Here

Monster movies can be fun. But when you're sitting there, scared out of your seat and loving every minute of it, you don't believe that the wild weirdos on the screen are real. If you did, you'd walk around in constant terror that lurking behind every other corner was a giant toad (or ant, or spider, or bicycle pump) waiting to capture you for its own (*heh heh heh*) evil purposes.

## Fears Kids Have

Okay, you don't believe everything you see in the movies or on TV. But you're probably afraid of some things. Here are some fears many kids have:

- Being lost or abandoned
- Being kidnapped
- Being attacked by a vicious dog (or other animal)
- Falling down and/or getting hurt
- Having a stranger break into the house

## How to Handle Fears

1. *If the fear is real, and you're in danger, act as quickly and calmly as possible.*

Someone is breaking into your house and your parents aren't home! Of course, you're frightened. But that doesn't mean you can't act. Your heart may be pounding, your palms may be sweating, and your knees may be knocking, but you can get to the phone to call the police or run out the back door to a neighbor's house. (For help on handling and preventing many kinds of dangerous situations, see SAFETY AND SECURITY.)

2. *If the fear is a real* possibility, *take precautions so that it won't happen.*

If you're afraid of getting lost, be sure you have very good directions before you set out. Take a map or written directions, if

necessary, or go with someone else the first time until you know your way.

3. *If the fear is about something that happens often, take extra precautions.*

If you're always burning yourself in the kitchen, you're probably being too careless. Find out what you're doing wrong, and correct it. Moving too fast? Slow down. Picking up hot things without pot holders? Use them. (See ACCIDENT PREVENTION for more pointers on avoiding accidents and injuries.)

4. *But if the fear is of something that is* very unlikely *to happen, talk it over with your parents to try to get to the root of the problem.*

If you're afraid of sharks — even when you're swimming in a river — it may be that you were so impressed by a scary story that you are not listening to your own good sense: you *know* sharks are not found in rivers.

5. *And if the fear is always there, or if you don't understand why you're afraid, it's really important to talk it over with your parents.*

Just discussing it often helps to overcome it, although this sometimes does take time. It also may be that you have a *phobia*.

## Phobias

People of all ages have phobias — fears of specific things, such as cats, snakes, planes, heights. Some phobias have special names:

*Claustrophobia* (the fear of being in closed-in places)

*Agoraphobia* (the fear of being in open spaces)

If you're afraid of a vicious dog who looks like he'd love to get his rather large paws on you, you don't have a phobia, you have a problem. Stay clear of that animal! But if you're afraid of all dogs, no matter how friendly, or how familiar, or how small, or how gentle they are, you may have a phobia. Your parent may want you to see a professional counselor, which simply means you'll be telling your problem to a person who's trained to help you get over it.

## Afraid of the Dark: Not for Kids Only

Why are so many people afraid of the dark? Maybe because:

- In the dark, you fall more easily or bump into things, so you could get hurt.
- It's more dangerous to be out after dark than in the daytime because crimes are more easily committed when no one can see what's going on.

These are real dangers, but they certainly can be avoided:

- Unless there's a power failure, you can simply turn on the lights to get rid of the dark. If you have to move about without light, do it carefully, feeling your way around — slowly.
- Try to avoid being out at night alone, as your parents have probably made quite

clear. If you have to go somewhere by yourself after dark, follow the precautions in the section on SAFETY AND SECURITY.

## Children's Fears

What do you do when you're taking care of a young child who comes to you and says, "I'm scared!"?

1. Don't laugh it off. No matter how silly it sounds, it's very real to that child.

2. Listen to the whole story, even if you think you know what you're going to hear, then talk to the child.

3. Try these techniques:

• If the child is convinced there's a fifty-foot snake (*ugh!*) under his bed, investigate the scene together, holding on to the child's hand. Then explain the odds of this being the case. When was the last time anyone found a fifty-foot snake *anywhere?* (The same is true for ghosts, monsters, and other assorted creepy things.)

• If the child is afraid his parents won't come back (many little kids are petrified of that), explain where they are and when they're returning. If it's really serious, and you know the child isn't putting you on, you could call the parents. But that's a last resort.

• If the child has a serious fear, all you can do is listen, be understanding, and then urge the child to talk it over with a parent. Remember, the child looks up to you and just may take your advice.

4. When they return, tell the parents what happened.

See also WORRYING.

# Fights

See ARGUMENTS.

 FIRE

## Fire!

If there's a fire in your home, or if you see or smell smoke, stay calm but act quickly. Alert everyone by shouting very loudly. If there's a child in your care, grab him or her and follow these steps:

1. **Get out as fast as possible!** But don't do anything that may endanger you.

• FEEL DOORS BEFORE OPENING THEM. If a door is hot, or if smoke is coming through the cracks, DO NOT OPEN THE DOOR: fire could be on the other side of it. Seal the cracks with wet towels or clothing, then open the window — break it if necessary! — and escape or scream for help.

• DON'T USE ELEVATORS if you live in an apartment building. Take the stairway.

• IF YOU HAVE TO GET THROUGH HEAVY SMOKE to escape, stay low, near the floor (smoke collects near the ceiling first). Cover your mouth (with a wet towel or cloth, if one is handy) and try not to breathe too deeply (the fumes can be poisonous).

**2. Call the fire department.** Pull the nearest alarm box or phone from a neighbor's. (Never call from a place where you might get trapped by fire or smoke!) Let the firemen know the exact location of the fire.

**3. Once you've escaped, don't go back for _anything!!_**

## Clothing Fires

If your clothing catches fire, _quickly_ do the following:

**1. Don't run.** (It fans the flame!)

**2. Lie down and roll over and over, or wrap yourself in a blanket, to smother the flames.**

**3. Remove clothing if you can, but do not pull it over your head.**

**4. Call a doctor.**

If someone else's clothing catches fire, follow the steps above, grabbing and pushing the person to the ground, if you must. Roll the person over, smothering the flames with whatever is handy: a coat, rug, blanket, drapes. If outside, use snow, dirt, sand. When flames are out, call for medical help — fast.

## Common Household Fires

Small fires of wood, paper, cloth, rubber, or plastic can be put out with water. For other types of fires, follow these instructions:

• _Food burning in stove._ Close the oven door. Turn off heat. The fire should go out in a minute or two.

• _Pan fire on stove._ Cover pan with a lid or a plate. Turn off the heat. The fire should go out in a minute or two. If the lid does not stop the fire, don't try to fight it — get away fast and call the fire department.

• _Electrical appliance._ First pull out the plug, or turn off the electricity. Extinguish fire with water _after_ the electricity is disconnected.

• _Smoke from television._ Stay clear! The picture tube might burst. If you can't unplug the set or turn off the electricity, call the fire department.

## Safety Measures

_Before_ a fire starts, you should know where a fire extinguisher is (and how it works) if your family has one. You should also be aware of the *safest* and *quickest* way to get out of your house in case of fire.

By the way, if your house or apartment doesn't have a smoke detector, this might be a great gift for your parents.

# FIRST AID

## In an Emergency

First aid is exactly what it says: the *first* thing you do to *aid* someone who's hurt. But it isn't usually meant to take the place of regular medical help — getting the person to a doctor or a hospital.

First aid can make a huge difference in how fast the person gets better, or whether or not there will be any permanent damage. It can even mean the difference between life and death!

Sounds scary. But luckily, there are some commonsense things you can learn *before* an accident or sudden illness happens. You don't have to be a Boy Scout to "be prepared," especially when it comes to first aid. Read this section carefully (maybe even twice) and pay special attention to the following:

- **Don't panic**
- **Get help**
- **Get out of danger**
- **Don't move the injured person unless absolutely necessary**
- **Treat first for bleeding, then for other problems**

## ☛ Don't Panic!

You've heard this so many times before, because it's really, really true. If you don't know anything else about a medical emergency, you can sometimes save the day by staying calm. That's easier said than done. So take a few deep breaths and tell yourself you're going to do the best you can. Besides helping you think more clearly, you'll make the injured person feel more confident. If that person thinks that

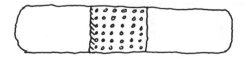

everything is under control and things will be okay, he/she will relax more and have a better chance to recover.

## Get Help!

Do whatever you have to do to make sure help is on the way. If you're alone, call for help as soon as you can safely leave the injured person. If there's no phone, get to the nearest person who can help. Of course, if there are other people with you, one can go for help while the others stay and give first aid. If the person is seriously injured, it's best to call for an ambulance with specially trained medical personnel, called EMTs (Emergency Medical Technicians) who can give on-the-spot treatment and transport the injured person safely.

## Get Out of Danger!

If the emergency is because of a fire, electrical shock, gas fumes, or other dangers, get the person — and yourself — away from the source of the danger *right away.* WARNING: This is the *only* time you ever move an injured person. At all other times, keep the person lying down until medical help arrives.

## First Things First!

*Breathing:* If a person stops breathing, every second counts. Get help immediately.

*Bleeding:* If breathing is okay, but there's bleeding, then this is at the top of your list. See the section on BLEEDING to learn how to control it.

*Shock:* If you've controlled the breathing and bleeding, and medical help still hasn't arrived, then treat for shock. In a first-aid situation, this means keeping the person warm and lying down. To find out more about SHOCK — what it is and how to treat it — read that section.

## Special Cases

For special first-aid situations, read the sections listed below. There are also some very special cases, such as epileptic, diabetic, or allergic attacks. The person may have information on the condition with him/her, or may be able to tell you about it. By the way, if you have any special medical problems of your own, be sure you have identification with you at all times stating the condition and telling what to do in an emergency. (Medic-Alert

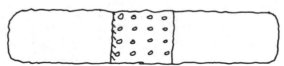

bracelets or necklaces are the best way to make sure you will be treated properly, if you have one of these problems.)

## First Aid for Minor Injuries

Sometimes, the term "first aid" is used to mean taking care of small injuries, like cuts and scrapes. (As you may have noticed, life is full of these little lumps.) If the hurt is very small, it should really be called "first-and-last aid," because you can take care of the problem easily and quickly, without having to see a doctor. It depends on how serious it is. You can find information on many common injuries in this book.

See the specific type of injury (BURNS, BROKEN BONES, BLEEDING, CUTS AND SCRAPES, TOOTH KNOCKED OUT, etc.) and FIRST-AID KITS.

‣ NOTES:

_____
_____
_____
_____
_____

# ❧ FIRST-AID KITS ❧

## What and When

First-aid kits are really important for medical emergencies. But they also come in handy for "life's little lumps." You'll probably find many useful items for first aid in your home already — in the medicine cabinet or in the kitchen. But it's a good idea to have everything in one place, so that when something happens, you don't have to waste time wondering where you left the bandages or the iodine.

Safety experts say that every home should have at least one first-aid kit, and, if possible, two for the house and one for the car(s). First-aid kits should be in places that everyone in the family knows about. This is no time for hide-and-seek. Everything should be clean, and organized so you can get to it quickly. It should *not* look like the bottom drawer of your friend's dresser or the back of your locker. If your family doesn't have a first-aid kit, perhaps you can make one for them.

A *basic* first-aid kit should include:
- *bandages*
- *sterile gauze pads and tape*
- *rubbing alcohol*
- *peroxide, Mercurochrome, or iodine*
- *an eyecup*

## What the Well-Dressed Kit Will Wear (and Why)

If you want to put together a super-duper deluxe version of a first-aid kit, here's our suggestion:

*Rx:* Check the "health" of your first-aid kit from time to time to make sure everything is in working order. Watch for expiration dates.

| *What* | *Why* |
|---|---|
| Sterile bandages (individually wrapped 4 × 4 gauze pads) | To dress cuts, stop bleeding |
| Adhesive tape (1 roll) | To hold bandages in place |
| Bandage adhesive strips (1 box) | To dress small cuts |
| Triangular bandages (4) and safety pins (12) | To make slings |
| Mild soap (1 bar) | To clean cuts, scrapes, burns |
| Peroxide or iodine (1 bottle) | To clean and disinfect cuts |
| Rubbing alcohol (1 bottle) | To sterilize tweezers |
| Tweezers (1 pair) | To remove splinters, bee stingers |
| Calamine lotion (1 small bottle) | To treat insect bites, poison ivy |
| Thermometer (1) | To check for fever |
| Cotton swabs (1 small package) | To clean cuts |
| Aspirin (1 small bottle) | To ease pain, reduce fever |
| Icebag or ice pack (1) | To prevent or limit swelling |
| Eyedropper and eyecup (1 of each) | To rinse eyes |
| Ipecac syrup (1 small bottle) | To treat poisoning |

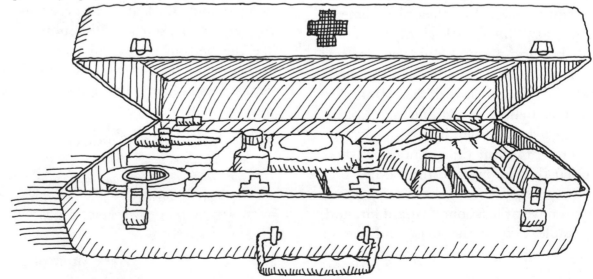

# 🐬 FITNESS 🐬

## A Lifetime Contract

Being "fit" means being in good physical condition, or being healthy. And if you think that's not a big deal, you better give it some more thought. Because it's the biggest deal you'll ever make — with yourself.

You don't have to become a fitness fanatic, but you should be aware of keeping in shape. After a while, it becomes a (good) habit. Before you know it, you'll be a healthy adult, because healthy kids have the very best chance of becoming healthy adults. But now is the time to make a lifetime contract.

What does it take to be fit? The basic ingredients are:

- Eating the right foods (see NUTRITION)
- Controlling your weight (see DIETING)
- Getting enough exercise (see EXERCISE)
- Getting enough rest and sleep

## Food, Preparing

See COOKING.

# 🐬 FOOD SHOPPING 🐬

## Don't Forget Your List

You've heard of "making a list and checking it twice"? That goes for shopping, too. It may sound like a bother, but it's a lot less trouble than getting to the supermarket and having your mind go blank as you stare at rows and rows of dog food and toilet-bowl cleaner and canned tuna fish and aluminum foil. It's also better than having to go back for something you forgot. (Like your list!)

Make the list reasonably neat. And make notes if there are special brands or sizes or quantities of things you're supposed to get. Ask what you should do if they don't have the *exact* size or brand. Forget it? Choose another one?

If you're shopping to help out your family, you'll get the information from a parent. Maybe he or she will even have the list done for you. Some people keep a running list of things they need in a handy spot. Also, if you're shopping so you can make a special recipe, make sure you write down *all* the ingredients. It's so easy to forget one little thing, and — especially in baking — one little thing can make a big difference.

Making a list gives you some idea of how much money you'll need, and how much stuff there'll be to carry. Unless you're going to charge it, make sure you have enough cash, and unless you're having it delivered, make sure you can handle it — either walking or bringing it back by bike.

Having a list in your hot little hand can also save you from the much-feared Supermarket Identity Crisis. (Oh, noooo . . .) You find yourself faced with sixty-seven brands of cereal, with names like:

*Filbert's Fluffy Flapjack Flips:* For Families Who Feel Fiercely About Fiber

*Sugar Sweet Softies:* Plenty Puffy!

*Macho Flakes:* Tender Hunks For Tough Honchos

You end up asking yourself, "Which cereal is really *me?*" when all you really wanted were cornflakes. Not only that, but what about all those offers for prizes and games and magic sets? It's too much! Yes, it is. So stay calm, don't be intimidated, and stick to the brands your family uses. If possible, avoid anything (including cereal) that is *loaded* with sugar and artificial ingredients. And think about it, how good could a magic set be if it can fit into a cereal box?

## Watch Out!

It's easy to be confused by all the choices, the signs, and the labels, but there are only two important things to beware:

- Look at the expiration date. When a package says, "Sell by Oct. 30," it won't be good after that date. *Don't buy it.* Get the package with the latest possible date, so that even if it sits around the refrigerator for a while, it will still be okay.
- Look at the container. If a can is swollen, really banged up, or rusty, or if a frozen package is very icy, don't buy it.

## Check It Out at the Checkout

Give your list one more look while you're waiting in line. Then be sure that everything you bought gets into your bags.

(Things get left out by mistake.) Check over your receipt and count your change. And don't be afraid to ask if something looks wrong.

## Meanwhile, Back at the Kitchen . . .

When you get home, put everything away as soon as you can. First things first: store the frozen food in the freezer, then put away the food that belongs in the refrigerator, then get everything else into its place in a cabinet or drawer. Follow any special procedures your family has for storing food, such as putting the eggs into those

little holders in the fridge, wrapping meat in clear plastic before putting it in the meat bin, storing veggies in the "crisper," or packing certain frozen foods in freezer paper.

Do this as soon as you get home. Juices get warm, frozen soups thaw out (and it's dangerous to refreeze any kind of frozen food), and you end up with a big mess in the kitchen, with things melted, mushy, and soggy. Besides, the sooner you put things away, the sooner you make yourself a snack. Anyone for Macho Flakes?

◗ NOTES:

_____
_____
_____
_____

# Fuses

See ELECTRICAL PROBLEMS.

 *Through*

## ✌ GAS FUMES ✌

### Check It Out!

If you smell even a slight odor of gas, open the windows right away and try to find out where the gas is coming from. Most probably, the fumes are coming from a gas stove. This happens when a burner is turned on but doesn't light, so that the gas just keeps coming out. (Sometimes this is because the pilot is out. If you don't know how and where to light the pilot, keep a window open and let your parent know about the problem as soon as she/he gets home.) *Turn off all burners.* Don't turn them back on until all the fumes are gone.

When you're searching for the trouble, do not use a lighted match or candle (when you find the gas leak, you could also find yourself in the middle of an explosion). If it's dark, try a flashlight.

If the odor is really strong, treat the situation as an emergency, and take these steps:

1. **Get everyone — including yourself — out** *immediately.*

2. **Call the fire department from a neighbor's house.**

3. **Turn the gas off,** *only* **if the turn-off valve is outside.**

If someone becomes ill from the gas fumes, get him outside, breathing fresh air, right away. Keep the person calm, quiet, and comfortably warm until medical help arrives.

♦ NOTES:

_____
_____
_____
_____
_____
_____
_____

## Getting Around

See BICYCLES, PUBLIC TRANSPORTATION, and SAFETY AND SECURITY.

# Grooming

See APPEARANCE.

# Hair Care

See APPEARANCE.

# HEAD INJURIES

## Bumps and Lumps

Most head injuries are nothing more than bumps on the head. And most people get their share of these. You don't have to do anything about them, unless you notice any of these "ifs":

• *If* the bump raises a lump, put some ice in a towel and hold it against the spot to keep the swelling down. Stop after fifteen to twenty minutes (we don't want anyone to get a case of frostbite!). Repeat every two to four hours for up to twenty-four hours, while you're awake.

• *If* the scalp is cut, use direct pressure to stop the bleeding: hold a sterile gauze bandage or a clean cloth against the wound and press gently. (See BLEEDING.)

• *If* the person is stunned or a little dizzy, get him/her to lie down and rest. Make the person comfortable, with a pillow or rolled-up jacket under the head. For the next few hours (and even days), be on the lookout for any signs of serious injury, like severe headaches, fainting, weakness, nausea.

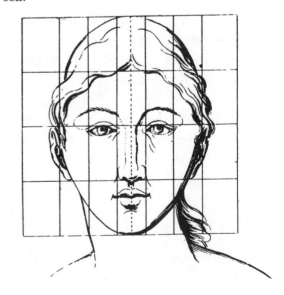

• **If** the person is unconscious, or is really drowsy or dizzy, or has a very bad head-ache, blurry or double vision, heavy bleeding, or begins to vomit, get medical help *right away!* It could be a concussion, fractured skull, or other major problem.

See also FIRST AID.

♦ NOTES:

---
---
---
---
---

# ❧ HEADACHES ❧

Headaches usually aren't serious, but they are signals that something is wrong. It could be stress, hunger, eyestrain, lack of sleep, allergies, or illness.

Until your parents get home, the best thing you can do for a "simple" headache is to relax. Go to your room (that's a sug-

gestion, not an order!), open the window, if it's not too cold outside, for some fresh air, and lie down for a while. If your head-ache was caused by being nervous or scared about something, relaxing like this might be all you need.

If you think your headache came on because you skipped lunch, have a snack. If you think it's from eyestrain, stop read-ing or watching TV. If it's from lack of sleep, take a nap. In other words, try to get rid of the cause of the headache, and the headache will probably go away, too. Don't take aspirin or any other pills with-out your parents' okay.

 ## When a Headache Is Serious

There are certain kinds of headaches that may be "signals" of something serious:

- A very sharp pain that comes on suddenly
- A headache that starts after a blow to the head or other head injury
- A headache combined with nausea, fever, or dizziness

If you have any of these kinds of headaches, *tell your parents immediately.*

Also tell them if you have headaches often. It may mean you need glasses (or a new prescription) or just that you've been reading in the wrong light. When you find out the cause, you can prevent most headaches. And prevention is the best kind of medicine.

▶ NOTES:

_____
_____
_____
_____
_____

## Homework

See SCHOOLWORK.

## ❧ HOSPITAL STAYS ❧

### Getting the Facts

The idea of going to the hospital is a little scary for anyone. The way to make it less scary is to learn as much as you can about what's going to happen while you're there. And you do this by asking questions:

- Why are you going to the hospital?
- What will be done?
- How long will it take?
- When will you be coming home?

You may not get the *exact* answers, but at least you'll have a good idea of what's going on. The worst thing is not knowing, because then you imagine all sorts of horrible things. And believe it or not, your parents may be more nervous than you are! If they don't understand something, ask them to try to find out about it. The more everyone knows, the less everyone worries.

And now the really big question:

- Will it hurt?

This is hard to answer, even for your doctor. It depends on many things, including how relaxed you are. But you can find out what you can generally expect. And remember, it won't last forever. It's like the

nervousness you feel at school on the day of a test. It goes away and you soon forget it. It helps to think about the fun things you're going to do when your stay is over.

## Getting Your Gear Together

In a way, it's like going to camp. But when you pack for a hospital stay, the less you take, the better. And you *don't* need a flashlight!

What you *do* need is:

1 bathrobe
1 pair of slippers
Brush or comb
Toothbrush
Books or magazines
1 or 2 small games

You could also take:

1 pair of pajamas (for when you're really sick of the hospital gown)
Clean clothes (for the day you go home)
Drawing pad and crayons or markers (if you're the artistic type)

But you definitely *don't* need:

5 pairs of anything
Anything really expensive or valuable

The first people you'll talk to will probably be in the admissions office. They usually ask a lot of questions and use big words. They're trying to find out if there's anything about you they should know — like if you're allergic to grapefruit, which they were planning to serve for breakfast the next morning. If you don't understand anything they ask, ask questions of your own. And there *is* something to look forward to at the end of all this: you get a plastic bracelet with your name on it. Big deal.

## Go to Your Room

There are three basic kinds of rooms in hospitals: *wards, semiprivate,* and *private.*

Wards usually have a lot of kids of all different ages. Everyone is there for different reasons — from appendicitis to broken legs. If you're in a ward, you'll have lots of company. But you also may have someone around who isn't very happy. Remember that everyone is there to get better, so try to find other cheerful souls — like yourself — to talk to.

Semiprivate rooms usually have from two to five people. It's like sharing a bedroom with your brothers and sisters.

Private rooms are for one person only — you.

Whatever kind of room you get, you've got to know:

- How — and what — to call the nurse (no, you don't yell, "Hey, Nurse!" Most hospitals have a buzzer or button to press. Find out where it is, and use it when you have to — and find out your nurses' names).

- How your bed works. Some hospital beds have cranks, and some have electric buttons. Most beds move in different positions, like raising the back so you can sit up in bed.

## Visiting Hours

Every hospital has different rules about this, and some are more strict than others. Ask your parents when they'll be coming and for how long, so there'll be no sur-

prises. Sometimes, people in the hospital think that they're being neglected, when it's actually very hard for their family and friends to get the time to visit them.

## Telephones, Televisions, and Other Frills

Things like telephones and televisions in your room cost extra money, so that's something your parents will have to decide about. But some hospitals have play-

rooms or television rooms you can use for free. The books and games you bring with you from home also don't cost anything extra, and can keep you just as amused.

## And Then There's the Food . . .

Well, yes, it probably will be yecchy. But there are some good things: you usually get a choice of menus, which you don't get at home. (And boy, is it tough choosing between whipped asparagus delight and poached toast on toast!) And people might bring you goodies (if it's allowed), so you'll probably get by very nicely.

 *Through*

## Where Does It Hurt?

If you're home alone and you begin to feel ill, the first thing you do is contact a parent or your doctor. That's fine, as long as you really are ill. But don't be too hasty: you might have a slight stomachache or headache that will go away very quickly, and you don't want to put your parent in a panic over nothing. (See HEADACHES and STOMACHACHES.)

If the pain is bad or if you think you have a fever, call a parent or a neighbor right away. Try to be specific about what's bothering you. Saying "I feel rotten" won't tell anyone what's wrong. Follow the directions you're given, which probably will be just to relax until someone gets there. *Don't* take any medicine unless you're instructed to do so.

## Rest Is Best

Suppose you're ill already, and you have to spend time at home, sometimes alone. You'll have directions to follow from your folks or your doctor (or both), and your own good sense to tell you what to do. For any illness, you need lots of rest in bed. Since you can't sleep all day and all night (or can you?), you can read, watch TV, draw, play cards or other games. Just don't make yourself tired, which is easier to do than you think, because you're not your usual healthy self. You may be surprised to find that when you're ill, even a short game of checkers can make you sleepy. So sleep. The more rest you get, the faster you'll get better.

## Gesundheit!

The most common illness you'll get is the common cold: runny nose, sneezing, aches, sometimes a sore throat or fever. Besides rest, colds are usually treated by drinking plenty of liquids, especially water and fruit juice. You may also be taking aspirin, cold medicines, cough syrup, or throat lozenges. If so, don't take more than the dosage that's been given to you by your doctor or parent. Sometimes your doctor may prescribe an antibiotic for your sore throat. In that case, don't take the medicine for *less* time than the

doctor tells you to take it, even if you're feeling better.

## How about Hay Fever?

If you have a chronic condition, such as hay fever, allergies, or asthma, you should have your medication handy all the time. When you're home alone and have an attack, you may be able to take care of it yourself. But tell your parents about it later. When you have an attack in class or when you're with a group of people, excuse yourself immediately to take your medicine. No one will think there's anything strange about this: many people have these conditions, including some famous athletes, actors, and musicians.

In time, you may "outgrow" your aller-gies. You may also be able to help stop your allergic attacks. Many illnesses, especially this kind, can be brought on or made worse by stress. Your job is to learn how to be more relaxed (see WORRYING). Also try to learn not to "fight" the attack once you've got it. Relax, take your medication (or follow your doctor's instructions for exercises such as deep breathing), and wait for the attack to pass. It will.

◆ NOTES:

_____
_____
_____
_____
_____
_____

When you're babysitting for an infant, you're really *baby*sitting. Infants are babies up to about eighteen months old, and they need special care. You might be on a babysitting job, or you might be minding your little brother or sister. Either way, there are some specific things you need to know about infants.

## For Crying Out Loud

The little dears do cry a lot, don't they? Don't forget it's their only way of "telling" you what's wrong. What's wrong is usually that they're 1) hungry, 2) wet, or 3) in pain (from something like an unfastened safety pin). So what do you do when a baby cries? You check to see if 1) it's feeding time, 2) the diapers need changing, or 3) a pin is open, or something else is hurting. One common source of pain for an infant is teething (you can ease the pain a little by rubbing his gums gently with your *clean* fingers).

## The Big Burp

Infants often cry because of stomach pain caused by gas. So if you're watching a baby, and have checked out all the other reasons he might be crying (sleepiness,

teething pain, an open pin, etc.), then try burping the baby. Babies can't burp themselves. Well, they do the actual burping, you just help it along. Hold the child upright against your shoulder and gently pat or rub his back. After a few minutes, you should hear the big burp, and the gas will pass.

## Feeding Time

You don't give an infant a slice of pepperoni pizza. That much you know. What and when you do feed him depends on the instructions you get from the parent.

*How* do you feed an infant? Very carefully. Put a bib on the baby and cover yourself — there is no way to avoid a few

spills during this process. Use a spoon, never a fork, and keep the food out of the baby's reach. Don't force him to eat if he doesn't seem hungry. But even if he is, you'll have to be patient. The amount of food that goes from the spoon into the baby will never be 100 percent. And, to bring up another point, babies sometimes vomit even when they're not sick. Just clean up, and tell the mother about it when she returns.

## Sleepytime

Babies usually sleep right after feeding. Stay with the infant while he's falling asleep, then check in on him every thirty minutes or so.

## Time for a Change

If you're expected to change diapers, make sure one of the parents shows you how. (Different kinds of diapers go on in different ways.) A special note: if safety pins are used, remember to keep them closed and out of the reach of the baby.

## Playtime

Since infants spend most of their time sleeping, eating, burping, and messing up their diapers, they don't have much chance to play. Anyway, they couldn't exactly run out for a quick game of softball. No, but they do like to have a little fun, mostly the "pat-a-cake," "peek-a-boo," and "this-little-piggy" kind of thing. Even tiny babies love attention, and playing these simple games, or holding them up to see themselves in a mirror, or singing softly, or just plain talking, is great.

Babies love to hear silly sounds like clucking noises or nonsense syllables — and that infant in your arms is one person who'll never tell you to be quiet. You can also "play" along with the baby, with mobiles hanging over the crib, or with soft toys you squeeze or squeak. Let the child fool around with your fingers, or explore your face and hair with his fingers. Just don't let an infant grab anything dangerous, including medicine, tiny things that can go into his mouth, or sharp objects such as those diaper pins mentioned already.

### Strolling Right Along

If you're asked to take the baby out for a walk, remember two things: push the carriage at a leisurely pace, and keep hold of it at all times.

### It's All in Your Hands

Infants are helpless little things, and you have to handle them carefully. Ask a parent to show you how, keeping in mind that very young babies can't hold their heads up by themselves. You have to support the infant's head with one hand and hold his body with the other. Do this — and everything else connected with infants — very gently.

See also BABYSITTING and BROTHERS AND SISTERS.

◆ NOTES:

_____
_____
_____
_____
_____
_____

# Injuries

See FIRST AID and specific type of injury.

## ∾ IRONING ∾

When in doubt, don't! Try to avoid wrinkles in the first place by taking clothes out of the dryer right away, or by hanging up hand wash while the clothes are wet and letting gravity do its job. If something is wrinkled, but clean, try hanging it up in the bathroom, especially when someone's taking a hot shower. The steam from the shower should do the trick. If all else fails, iron.

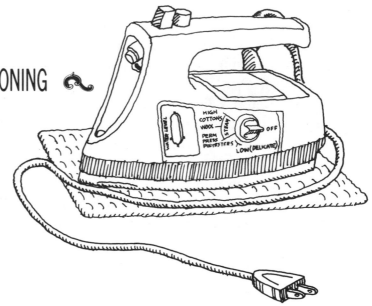

It's hard to iron something really well, and it takes practice. But even if you can't iron a shirt perfectly the first time, at least you can make sure you don't burn it. Set the iron for the material you're working on (check the label). If you're not sure what it is, use a low setting to be safe. The general rule is that light, soft material like nylon needs very little heat, and that heavy strong material like denim needs higher heat. You can also prevent burning by not letting the iron stop too long on one spot. You don't have to go as fast as the speed of light, but keep the iron moving! To make life easier, sprinkle the clothes with a little water. Or use a steam iron.

☛ *SAFETY TIPS:*

• Irons are hot, and they can burn you as well as the clothes, so handle them with care (and respect). Steam can burn, too, so be doubly careful with steam irons.

• Stand the iron up on its end when it's at rest, and unplug it when you're finished.

• Don't put away a hot iron in its box or closet right away. Let it cool first on the stove or on any other nonburnable surface.

See also APPLIANCES.

◗ NOTES:

_____
_____
_____
_____

## ✧ JEALOUSY ✧

They don't call it the green-eyed "monster" for nothing. Jealousy is like a monster: it can get bigger and uglier and more out of control all the time, *if you let it.*

Is it possible never to be jealous? Nope. Everyone has at least a twinge of it sometimes. This feeling is very human. *Very* human. Just don't go around actually hurting the people you're jealous of.

You may not be able to destroy the "monster" altogether, but you can learn to keep it in its place. For instance, has it ever happened to you that you've been secretly jealous of someone, and at the same time, that person has been jealous of you? (*She* may have the lead in the play, but *you* always get the best grades. Or vice versa.)

Instead of thinking so much about other people's brains or brawn or looks or luck, concentrate on your own good points, and on making yourself the best you can be. Use our checklist to remind yourself of what you've got going for you:

- ☐ athletic skill
- ☐ mechanical ability
- ☐ intelligence
- ☐ creativity
- ☐ musical talent
- ☐ good looks
- ☐ all of the above (!)

You take these things for granted because you've always had them. But if you can win a race, fix a clock, solve a problem, paint a picture, play a guitar, or just plain dazzle people with your big beautiful eyes, then someone out there, at this very moment, is jealous of *you.*

## ✧ JOBS — FOR YOU ✧

### Kid for Hire

Before you can do a job, you've got to get it. You can get hired by answering an ad in the local newspaper or a notice on the bulletin board at the supermarket. Or, someone may just give you a job. But what if you want to work and you don't have any prospects? Well, it *does* pay to advertise. Here are some ways to do it:

- *Word-of-mouth publicity.* Tell your family, friends, and neighbors that you're looking for a job, and the kinds of things you'd like to do. Even if they don't have a job for you, they may know someone who does. And remember, the best advertisement of all is doing a good job. The word gets around.

• *Written messages.* Write your name, phone number, what you do, when you're available, and your rates on pieces of paper. If you can use a copy machine, make lots of copies. If not, keep the message short and sweet and write it out by hand. Hang up the flyers in places like grocery stores, pet shops, churches, temples, apartment building bulletin boards, and schools. If you're the artistic type, you can make posters instead of flyers, adding a picture or two to catch people's attention.

• *Group help.* Organizations like the 4-H Club, the YMCA/YWCA, Boys Club, or Campfire Girls can sometimes help you find a job.

## A Word of Warning

Be very careful when you answer an ad, or when someone you don't know answers your ad. Find out about the person before you take the job. You might be able to talk to someone who worked for the person before, or get a parent to help you get some information. Don't go into a strange neighborhood or into an apartment house which is new to you unless you have an adult along to meet the person. And never

agree to take a car ride with a stranger to the place where you're supposed to be working. If you feel uncomfortable about the job, don't take it.

## Doing Your Thing(s)

There are many kinds of jobs for kids. Choose from the following selections, or think of something yourself. The important thing is to find out which services are needed in your area, and which you can do best and enjoy the most. Here are some ideas:

*NOT JUST "SITTING AROUND"*
You've heard of babysitting. But what about *plant* sitting? Or *house* sitting? Or *pet* sitting? The idea is basically the same. Something needs watching to keep it safe. Whether it's a child, a plant, a house, or a pet, your job is to make sure everything is all right.

Plant sitting usually means simply watering plants for someone who's going to be away. Without water, the plants would

die. But too much water is no good either. Get directions on how much water each plant gets and how often. You'll find more on the subject of plants under PLANT CARE.

House sitting may mean simply collecting the mail or newspapers when a family is away. Or you might be asked to

stay in the house for a few hours each evening. The whole idea of this is to make the house look occupied, so that no one will try to break in.

Pet sitting is a lot like babysitting, except that pets are usually easier to get along with than kids. All pets need are

food, a clean cage, bowl, box, or whatever. Maybe a walk around the block, and a little love. But do get specific instructions for each pet and follow them exactly. People really love their pets and want them treated with tender loving care.

### THE PET SET

If you love animals too, you might want to do more than just pet sitting. For example, you could be a dog walker. (Or dog runner. Or dog jogger.) Many people, espe-

cially in cities, find that their dogs don't get enough exercise. And you can help. It's best to walk only one dog at a time, and

always keep it on a leash. Don't let the dog loose in a park or a vacant lot, or tie it to a tree or fence. More about dog walking can

be found in the section on PET CARE. In that section, you'll also find some tips on

washing a dog, if you decide you want to become a dog washer. But do it only if you know the dog.

### MAKING GREEN WITH GREENS

If you'd rather talk to the trees than deal with fleas, you might become the friendly neighborhood gardener. You can mow lawns, pull up weeds, or rake leaves. Make sure you know the dandelions from the daffodils, and how to work a lawnmower or rake. Otherwise, you could end up mowing leaves, raking weeds, or pulling up lawns. And it's not nice to fool around with Mother Nature.

### GROWING UP GREEN

If you're really good at growing things, you can make a business out of it. Most books on plants tell exactly how to do it, but the idea is to take a small clipping

from one plant to start another. With just a few plants, you can grow many more, planting the clippings in small pots, cans, even paper cups. When they're grown, you can sell them to your neighbors or set up a stand.

You can even start plants from seed. Seeds are not expensive, but you have to follow the directions on the package and

give the young plants plenty of care. If you plan ahead, you can plant seeds in bright-colored gourds in the spring, then sell your plants in the fall for Halloween or Thanksgiving decorations.

Herbs can be grown from seeds or cuttings near a window where there's bright

light a few hours a day. Cooks love herbs, such as dill, basil, mint, and chives. You should be able to find a market for home-grown herbs, especially in the city.

### BE A PAPERPERSON?

Some kids find that paper routes work very well for them. Others think they're too much work and too little money. Check your local paper for the details of delivering papers in your area. Then make up your own mind.

### SALE ON

Are you a born salesperson? Here's one way to find out: go through your belongings to find things you no longer want or

need. Then hold a sale. You can sell comic books, records, books, toys, almost anything. Join forces with some other enterprising kids and have a "garage sale." Make sure you know the value of things so you won't sell them too cheaply. And always check with your folks. They just may not want you to sell that brand-new sweater Aunt Agnes knitted — even if it does itch.

You can also sell lemonade or brownies (see our recipes under COOKING) and other goodies by setting up a stand and making a sign. Just make sure that the price you charge is more than what it costs you to make them.

### *TUTORING YOUR OWN HORN*

Do you play the trumpet pretty well? Are you a whiz at math? The best kicker on the soccer team? You might be able to become a tutor or a coach to help other kids who are having trouble with the thing you do best.

### *MORE KID STUFF*

Many parents would love it if you started a school pick-up service, meeting little kids at school and seeing them home. Or you could set up a Saturday shopper sitting center. (Say *that* fast ten times!) Put aside a few hours in the afternoon and have parents drop off children while they run their errands. If there'll be more than two or three kids at a time, share the job with a friend or friends. And be sure to read the sections on BABYSITTING and ENTERTAINING CHILDREN.

### *PARTNERS*

Besides the sitter center, many jobs can be a little too much to do alone, so you might try teaming up with a partner. Some of these jobs are snow shoveling, car washing, painting. You could also use a partner to run a delivery service on your bikes, or a laundry service (see the section on LAUNDRY).

*RENT-A-KID*

You say you're an all-purpose kid with lots of uses, talents, and energy? Boy! Is there a job for you! You become a "Rent-a-Kid" by advertising the things you can do. Things like

- mowing lawns
- running errands
- picking up cleaning or laundry
- washing dishes
- house cleaning
- anything else you can think of!

Many older people have trouble doing these things and would be glad to have a helping hand. But even younger people could use this service because they're too busy to get all their chores done. This goes double for parents with young children.

## The Price Is Right

When kids get jobs they often wonder how much they should charge. That depends. Some things, like babysitting or mowing lawns, have a "going rate." You can find out what other people your age are getting for those jobs, and ask for about the same.

Of course, if you think you have something extra to offer — like lots of experience with kids or many satisfied lawn-

owning customers — then ask for a little more. You might not get it. But most people will respect you for thinking so highly of yourself.

Sometimes, it's hard to know what to charge. Suppose you grow herbs or flowers and sell them. There's no "going rate" among the other kids for that. But there is the local market or flower shop. Find out what your products cost at those places, and this time, charge a little less. You want to give the person a reason to try your "brand" instead of the store's. After a while, if your things are really good, they'll be in demand and you can raise your prices.

## One More Thing . . .

Whenever you're on a job, let your parents know where you are and when you expect to be home.

See also MONEY.

# ∾ KEYS—LOST ∾

If you lose your keys, and no one is home, go to a friend's or neighbor's home and call your parent. Let him/her know what

happened. And be patient: you might have to wait until someone gets home to let you in.

If you know there's an extra set of keys with a neighbor, superintendent, or in a hidden spot, by all means use them. But call your parent anyway.

If you lose your keys (especially if you suspect they were stolen) along with some means of identification (your name and/or address and telephone number), *don't go home,* even if you know where extra

keys are hidden. Instead, go to a neighbor's home and call your parent immediately. He/she may want to have the locks changed quickly so an intruder can't enter your home.

See also SAFETY AND SECURITY.

♦ NOTES:

_____
_____
_____
_____
_____

# ✤ LAUNDRY ✤

## Laundry: By Machine

You've already taken the *Appliance Tour* (see page 15), right? Then read on.

Wrong? Go back to APPLIANCES, and have your parent give you the tour so you'll know how to run the washer and dryer.

### *STEP ONE: HOW TO SUCCEED IN LAUNDRY WITHOUT TURNING THE UNDERWEAR GRAY*

When it comes to machine washing, there are two kinds of clothes. No, not dirty and clean. *All* clothes for the laundry are dirty. The answer is light and dark. (The lightest light is white, and the darkest dark is black.)

So what's the big deal? The big deal is that if you wash light things, like white socks, along with dark things, like jeans or plaid shirts, the light stuff can pick up color from the dark stuff. More often than not, the colors from many things mix, so what you get is yellowish, yecchy gray. Not a great color, especially for underwear or T-shirts that started out being bright white.

Sometimes it's even worse. The red from your football jersey runs into the white pillowcase, turning it pink. Nothing wrong with a pink pillowcase, except that it isn't pink all over, just in big, blotchy blobs. And it doesn't match the rest of the bed. Oh, well, you could try washing the sheets and the other pillowcase with the same red jersey . . . Good luck!

One more "sorted" detail: you might want to separate the lint-givers of the laundry world (fluffy stuff like your yellow terry-cloth robe, or your kid brother's teddy bear) from the lint-getters (dark materials that pick up — and show — every tiny piece of lint). A little lint will usually come off in the dryer, but a lot of lint can really hang in there.

## STEP TWO: SHAKE IT!

No, this isn't a new disco dance. It's a very practical step. (Get it? Dance? Step?) Shake out loose dirt, empty all the pockets, and take off any jewelry, pins, or belts that wouldn't do too well in the washing machine.

## STEP THREE: TOO MUCH

Okay, you've got your basic pile of laundry — all nicely sorted and shook — and you're ready to go. The next step is to put the clothes into the machine. Sound easy? It is. Except for one little thing: don't overload. At best, you won't get really clean clothes. At worst, you can create a small flood. So, the question is, how much is too much? Generally, the machine should be a little more than half full. When in doubt, read the instructions on the machine itself. But *never* cram any machine right up to the very top. And spread the clothes evenly in the machine.

## STEP FOUR: THE DOPE ON SOAP

Now put in the detergent. Again, don't overdo it. A mountain of overflowing suds can cause all kinds of clean-up problems. The idea of cleaning up soapsuds may sound silly, but it's no joke when it happens. Here again, it pays to read the directions. The package of laundry soap or detergent will tell you exactly how much to use. Enough to get the clothes clean, but not enough to turn your laundry room into a floating disaster area.

## STEP FIVE: HOT STUFF

Your next move is to set the machine and start the wash. One setting that might confuse you is water temperature. Should you use HOT, WARM, or COLD? That depends. For white things, you usually use HOT water. For everything else, use WARM or COLD. The package of detergent will give you good advice, but you should also check out the labels of your clothing. If a label reads:

> *Machine Wash*
> *in Warm Water*

you know that it's fine to throw it into the machine, but that you shouldn't use HOT water.

Of course, if the label happens to say:

> *Hand Wash*
> *in Cold Water*

you should skip this section entirely and go directly to *Laundry: By Hand*, page 156. (Do not pass *Go* or collect two hundred dirty socks.)

Besides the problem of colors fading and running into each other, some things shrink in hot water. A lot. That's another

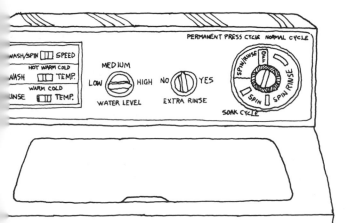

reason to read the labels. It's pretty frustrating to turn your favorite sweater into the perfect coat — for your hamster. Your pet may think you're hot stuff, but nobody else will. Guaranteed!

### STEP SIX (MAYBE): EXTRAS

If your family uses a *fabric softener,* find out when you're supposed to put it in by reading the instructions. Some softeners are added at the beginning, some during the rinse cycle, and some (the paper kind) in the dryer.

*Bleach* is sometimes used to make things whiter or brighter, or to fade jeans. Make sure it's safe to use bleach on the clothes you're washing. Some things, like pure wool socks, will turn yellow instead of white (not cool). Even if bleach is safe for the fabric, never put it directly on dry clothes . . . unless you want your favorite sweatshirt to have that new "Swiss Cheese Look."

### STEP SEVEN (FOR SURE!): JUST WAIT

Always wait until the machine stops (after the spin-dry cycle) before you take the clothes out of the washer and put them into the dryer.

### STEP EIGHT: TRY DRYING

Try not to overheat or overdry your clothes. Most materials shouldn't be dried using the hottest setting. And even those that are, like jeans or towels, shouldn't take too long. If you're not sure about a temperature setting, choose the lower one. And if you're not sure how long it will take, try it for a short time, then give it more time, if needed. After a while, you'll know about how much time things take. So be ready to take them out of the dryer *as soon as* they're ready. (The rule is: get 'em dry and get 'em out.) Leaving them in there, just sitting around in a bunch, makes them wrinkled. You might even have to (ARRGH!!) *iron* something. (See IRONING.) As you take each item out of the dryer, fold it neatly before putting it away.

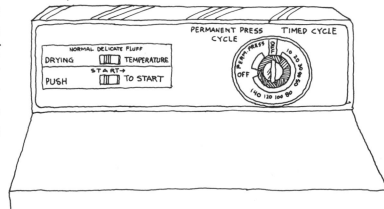

## Laundry: By Hand

Some things can't be done in the machine. And sometimes, you've only got a few things to do and don't want to waste water and electricity. You can save your own energy by using a special product for soaking clothes in cold water. (Follow the directions on the container.) Or, use a liquid dishwashing soap in cold, warm, or hot water, depending on the material. Remember, some things fade or shrink in hot water. And don't use too much soap — one quick squirt should do it. If something is really dirty, wash it out two times instead of using twice as much soap. It's really hard to rinse out all those suds, especially in a small sink.

Hang up shirts, pants, skirts, and dresses on hangers. (Want to know a trick even your mom might not know? If you're using wire hangers, use two or three at a time and you won't end up with points at the shoulders.) Sweaters and T-shirts stretch and get droopy if you hang them up, so spread them out flat on a towel. Cover them with a second towel if you think your pet might be tempted to sit on them. Small stuff, like underwear or socks, can be draped over hangers or on the towel racks by the shower or bathtub. Make sure none of your laundry is dripping on the floor.

## A Special Note about Laundry: How to Avoid Doing So Much in the First Place

You like the sound of this one, don't you? The only trouble is that it means doing something you hate almost as much as doing the laundry (maybe more!): hanging up your clothes. But if you put your things away on hangers or hooks or in drawers as soon as you take them off, they won't get so wrinkled (or dirty) and you won't have to wash them so often. (See CLOTHING CARE.) Look at it this way: while you're saving yourself work on the laundry, you'll also be cleaning up your room. And, best of all, you won't have to read all those directions!

▶ NOTES:

_____
_____
_____
_____
_____
_____

## Light Bulbs

See ELECTRICAL PROBLEMS.

## ∽ LONELINESS ∾

When you're feeling lonely, you're not alone. Everyone feels lonely sometimes. So, at the exact moment when you're feeling lonely, many other people are feeling the same way. One way to cure the problem:

• *Go out and find someone (maybe someone who's lonely too) to do things with.*

Here are some other ideas:

• *If there aren't many kids where you live (or even if there are), try making friends with an adult.*

Some grownups are lots of fun. And even those who don't play basketball or roller-skate may be very good storytellers — or good listeners.

• *When you're with people, make the most of it.* Join in on the activities at school that you enjoy, even if you're feeling a little shy. (Don't worry: you're not alone there, either. Many people, even famous stars like Elton John and Carol Burnett, were very shy when they were kids.) If you're active much of the time, you'll make many friends. You'll also find that you won't mind being alone some of the time. You might even enjoy it.

## Being Alone vs. Being Lonely

What you do when you're alone is very important. If you sit around and mope, or watch hours and hours and hours of television, and keep complaining about having nothing to do, you'll end up feeling very down. But being alone is not the same thing as being lonely. Try doing some of these things when you're by yourself, and you may have too much fun to be lonely:

• Practice a sport (shoot baskets, hit tennis balls against a wall, swing that bat).

- Do a chore or a job (clean up, cook up a storm, water the petunias).
- Watch a good TV show (you might learn something).
- Read a good book (or write one!).
- Play with a pet (if you have one).
- Work on a hobby (why not get one?).

There still may be times when you feel lonely, but don't let it bother you too much. It's part of life. It just doesn't have to be a very big part if you're an active person.

See also BOREDOM.

## MANNERS

You know it's good manners to say "Please" and "Thank you." But sometimes, you're in a new situation and you're not sure what you're supposed to do. The thing to remember is that manners are based on simple consideration of others. Use your own good sense, and you'll do the right thing. For example:

- When your cousin, Osgood, is really exhausted and trying to sleep, it's not good

manners to blow a trumpet in his ear (tubas are not recommended, either, but that's another story).

- When your Aunt Tessie has worked long and hard to serve you a super spaghetti dinner, it's good manners to wait for her to be seated, not to slurp up the strands in a single surge of suction before she hits the chair.
- And when Mr. Hocknell, from down the street, says "Hello" to you one morning, it's good manners to return the greeting rather than to eat his umbrella.

It's all logical. It's all basically easy. There's even a rule, known as The Golden Rule, which sums it up: "Do unto others as you would have others do unto you."

### But What about All Those Forks and Spoons?

There is one kind of situation concerning manners that can make anyone a little nervous. You're invited to dinner, and suddenly you're faced with unfamiliar-

looking food (oysters? artichokes? anchovies?) or many utensils placed alongside your plate (at home, you get a knife and fork, and a spoon if you're lucky). *Gulp.* You don't want to make the wrong move and make a fool of yourself.

Relax. There's a very easy way to handle this. Take your time, and watch. Notice how other people are eating the food, and which spoons and which forks they're using. This is a good strategy for three reasons:

1. You'll find out what you're supposed to do.

2. It's "good manners" to wait until the person at the head of the table starts to eat before you do.

3. You won't eat too quickly, which is not only bad manners, but bad for your digestion.

> *Don't be intimidated by a new situation,* at the table, or anyplace else. If you don't know what is proper, and you can't imitate someone else, then simply ask about it. Most people will respect you for having the courage to do this. At least, you'll find out what to do for the next time.

But back to the table. And a few basic rules you probably already know:

- Put your napkin on your lap as soon as you sit down.
- Keep your elbows off the table.
- When cutting your meat, don't let your elbow fly out into someone else's plate — or face.

- Only eat with your fingers if it's something like chicken, and everyone else is doing it.
- Say, "Please pass the potatoes," instead of reaching way across the table.

- Take only as much as you think you can eat: otherwise, you'll end up leaving most of the food, and it will look as if you don't like it.
- If you *don't* like it, eat as much as you can manage, with as little fuss as possible.
- Take human bites, and chew with your mouth closed. Otherwise, it looks gross.

## All Right, What *Else* Do I Have to Do?

Since *The Official Kids' Survival Kit* is not an etiquette book (aren't you glad?), we're not going to give you a complete list of everything you'll ever need to know about manners. But you should be aware of these rules:

- When visiting friends, act like the considerate, civilized person you are. Don't bang on the door, lean on the bell, yell at the top of your lungs (or the top of the stairs, or both), or go running through the house leaving a trail of broken glass and chipped furniture.
- When you sleep over, be a good guest. Offer to help out with dinner, or the dishes, or the garbage — or *something*. At the very least, make up your own bed and pick up your clothes. Don't borrow things without asking, raid the refrigerator, or hog the bathroom.
- When you have friends over, make them feel at home. Show them around, give them something to eat or drink (for good ideas,

see COOKING), and have something planned to do.

• When your family has friends over, try to make your parents proud by introducing yourself and acting a little interested in meeting their guests. This, and a few well-placed smiles, can take all of about forty-five seconds, and can score many, many points on the home front. (Even if someone acts like a real jerk and slobbers over you with stories of when you were a baby, be cool and act polite.)

• At family gatherings, you should do all of the above, but be around more — as much as you can, in fact — so as not to hurt anyone's feelings. Hanging out in your room the whole time is *not* the height of politeness.

• When someone has given you a present, or has done something special like having you stay overnight, send a little thank-you note. It doesn't have to be fancy or long. Even something like

will do!

## ✋ MICROWAVE OVENS ✋

Even if you know exactly how your family's microwave oven works, never, *never* use it if the door is open, warped, or damaged in any way. If you do, you can be exposed to harmful radiation that may be leaking out.

Other things you should know about the microwave oven:

• *Don't* operate it when it's empty.

• *Don't* cook with anything that contains metal: metal cookware, metal handles on cookware, etc. Use aluminum foil only as directed.

- *Don't* cook any food that is airtight — hot dogs, potatoes, tomatoes, food in closed plastic bags — without opening it or puncturing it with a fork. Steam can build up in airtight foods, causing them to burst and splatter inside the oven.

See also APPLIANCES.

◗ NOTES:

_____
_____
_____
_____
_____
_____
_____

# ∿ MONEY ∿

## Money Matters

It's a good idea to start working on a healthy attitude toward money. Money is *not* the "root of all evil"; in fact, it can be useful. If you want to start earning money, read the section on JOBS — FOR YOU. This section is about spending and saving money: using your dollars and good sense.

## Decisions, Decisions

Advertisers spend enormous amounts of money to get you to buy things, some of which you need, some of which you don't, some of which are good for you, some of which aren't. To complicate things, the government has begun to warn you about some of the things advertisers are advertising. And on top of all that, your parents may be telling you something different about many products.

Well, if it's your money you're spend-ing, then you have to make the decisions. Here are some guidelines to help you choose wisely:

### DON'T PLAY NAME GAMES

It's fun to buy something that all the kids at school have: a certain kind of jeans, shirt, or bag. That's fine — sometimes. Just don't think that you *always* have to get what everybody else gets. And don't be fooled into thinking that something is good just because it has the "right" label. You don't need a designer name; you have one of your own. What you do need is something that is priced right, fits right, and is well made.

### DON'T LET THE "STARS" GET IN YOUR EYES

Everyone has made this mistake at least once. You see something on TV or in a

Nothing fits me like my GRUBBIES!

magazine being shown by your favorite star or a glamorous model, and you just *have* to have it. If you can only get this product, you'll never have another problem as long as you live. *Sigh.* It never works that way. You won't turn into Super Kid because you buy *anything*. You may be in for a big disappointment, and you'll surely be in for a loss of money. Before you buy anything, make sure you're getting it for the right reasons: because you need it or want it, because it's beautiful or valuable or will help you. But not because you think it's magically going to change you into the star who's selling it.

## TRY BEFORE YOU BUY

When you're buying something, haste *does* make waste. So take your time and check out the product. Ask to try it out in the store, so you'll know how it works — and *if* it works. It could be broken.

## SHOP AROUND

Before you buy something, you might want to check out a few stores to see if you can get the same thing for less money, or if there's something you like even better.

## BEWARE OF BARGAINS

So, Bartholomew's Bargain Boutique has a special on yo-yos this week, eh? You can get a hundred yo-yos for only fourteen ninety-five! Hold on. What are you going to do with a hundred yo-yos? Start a yo-yo team? Look. A bargain is only a bargain if you need it.

## KNOW HOW TO SAY "NO"

Never feel forced into buying anything you don't want or can't afford. (Ask your-

self, "Do I really need another _____?")
And don't let a snooty salesperson make
you feel "small" if you don't buy the most
expensive thingamajig in the store. Remember, a salesperson's job is to help you
because you're the customer. You have the
right to ask questions, be choosy, and to
say no if you decide not to buy.

*SALES SLIPS SLIPS*
Don't forget the sales slip, which most
stores give you automatically, because it's
the only thing that proves you bought the
product. Don't throw it away until you're
sure you're pleased with your purchase. If
not, you can usually bring it back to the
store and get your money back.

Notice the word *usually*. Sometimes,
you'll see "final sale" on the slip. That
means you can't return your purchase.
Sometimes, you can return it but you
can't get your money back — you get a
credit and can buy something else in that
store.

Being able to return merchandise is one
of the reasons to shop at the good old reli-
able stores your family and neighbors use.
This kind of store will give refunds or cred-
its, and places like the new and exciting
Fly-by-Night NicNac Nook might not.

*TRIAL AND ERROR*
Don't feel too bad if you make a mistake
when buying something. We all do. Just
try not to make the same mistakes over
and over.

## Fix It First

Before you rush out to buy something
new, see if you can fix the old thing that
needs replacing. Maybe you don't need a
new bike. It could be slow because the tires
aren't properly inflated. (See the section
on BICYCLES.) Or maybe that old white
T-shirt just needs a little soaking in detergent and bleach. (See the section on LAUN-
DRY.) If you can fix an old thing, you may
be able to save the money you would have
spent on the new thing. Then, you can
buy something else, or put the money
away for something you will want in the
future.

## Keep On Walkin'

Whenever you can, try walking or biking
to where you're going instead of taking
buses or trains (or asking someone to take
you by car). You'll save money on fares,
help keep yourself in tip-top condition,
and help your country conserve energy.

## Safe, Not Sorry

Try not to lose money — or the things you buy with money. First of all, never send cash through the mail. If it gets lost or stolen, you have no proof that you sent it. (Good-bye, set of South American stamps. Good-bye, four ninety-eight.) Always send a money order, which you can get at the post office, or a check, if your parents want to arrange it.

Keep your money and your possessions in safe places, and don't leave things lying around in public places, like parks or playgrounds. If you have a game or piece of equipment you really like, write your name on it. That way, if it's lost, it may be returned. Losing things is losing money. Think of it that way and you'll be a little safer, and a lot less sorry.

## Making Money with Money

It's a good idea to invest some of your money in things that earn money. You can buy supplies for things you make and sell, like seeds for plants. Or brushes for your fence-painting business. This is similar to what adults do with their extra money (if they have any). They buy land or invest in businesses or the stock market.

In fact, if you saved enough money, you could buy stocks for yourself. Stocks are pieces of a company, and once you own even a single share of stock, you own a piece (usually a very small piece) of that company. If you're under eighteen, you need an adult to actually buy and sell the stocks, but they are in your name. You can buy any amount of stock, but you probably should have at least a hundred dollars saved up to start your *portfolio*, your collection of stocks. Remember, investing money like this is *not* a sure thing. You could make money, but you could lose some, too.

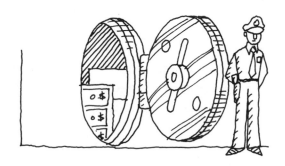

If you want to play it safe, put your savings into a bank. No, not a piggy bank. That may be cute, but it doesn't pay *interest*. A savings bank does. That means that every dollar you put in the bank earns a few cents each year. It can add up.

See also ALLOWANCE.

 Through

# ❧ NOSEBLEEDS ❧

If you get a nosebleed, stay calm. Sit up in a chair with your head in a normal upright position. Don't lie down or tilt your head back. Now, with your finger, press the nostril that's bleeding against the center of the nose. If both nostrils are bleeding, pinch the nostrils together with your thumb and index fingers. About five minutes of this direct pressure should help. If it doesn't, put a cold wet towel or ice pack across the bridge of the nose.

Nosebleeds usually aren't terribly serious, but they're no laughing matter. So don't laugh, talk, cough, blow your nose, or walk around. This might cause the nose to bleed even more, or get it going again if it has stopped.

If the bleeding is very heavy, or if it doesn't stop after about fifteen minutes, call your parent or doctor. If the nosebleed is the result of an injury to your nose, see FIRST AID.

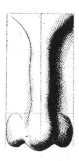

Follow these same steps if a child you're taking care of gets a nosebleed.

◆ NOTES:

_____
_____
_____
_____
_____

# ❧ NUTRITION ❧

The biggest stumbling block that comes between many kids and sound nutrition is letting sweets and junk foods become the main part of their diets. This is especially

true for kids who fix some of their own meals and/or are into heavy snacking.

Sugar is the main culprit. Many foods we eat today are loaded with it, and even "innocent-looking" things like canned soups, cheese spreads, and ready-made spaghetti sauces can contain sugar. (Did you know that catsup has sugar in it?) Here's a list of foods that contain a lot of sugar: • *candy* • *cake* • *pie* • *cookies* • *ice cream* • *soda* (except the diet kind) • *milk shakes, chocolate milk, hot chocolate* • *fruit punches* (with added sugar) • *cereal* (the kind with sugar added) • *sugar itself* (put on cereal, fruit — anything!).

Look over the list and see how many portions of these foods you've eaten in the past twenty-four hours. One? Two? Forty-seven? If your answer is two, you may be eating too much sugar. If it's three or more, you certainly are.

## What Can You Do with a Sweet Tooth?

Keep it under control by doing this:

• *Be aware of how much sugar you're eating, and set some limits.* If you had cake for dessert at lunch, and a bowl of ice cream after school, skip dessert at dinner. If you're having chocolate-chip cookies, pass up the sweet punch and have some milk instead. (It tastes better with cookies anyway.)

• *Check out the labels of foods you buy, and don't get too many things with sugar added.*

• *Get the knack of snacking.* Instead of sweets, try things like fruit, nuts, cheese, hard-boiled eggs, or yogurt. You'll probably develop a taste for these things: they taste good.

*What about Other Snack Foods?*

Even if you're not into sweets (lucky you), you may like potato chips, pretzels, popcorn, and things like that. These foods are not all bad. Some of them even have good things going for them (potato chips have potatoes, popcorn has corn). The trouble is that they're not good for you in large quantities — they contain too much fat and they may spoil your appetite.

If you have an occasional (small) bag of chips, no problem. But, as you know, it's hard not to overdo it, and when these foods begin to take over your diet (and your life!), watch out. The best way to keep this from happening is to follow the advice in the Sweet Tooth section: whenever you can, substitute fruit and other good foods for these "goodies."

## Your Own Balancing Act

As for "fast foods" such as burgers and fries, the thing to remember is that your diet must have a *balance* to it. That hamburger, toasted bun, and french fries are simply not enough. Your body needs a *variety* of foods to keep it healthy. Foods like:
• *fruit* • *vegetables* • *milk and milk products* • *cheese* • *lean meat* • *poultry* • *fish* • *eggs* • *whole-grain cereals and breads.* So if you ate *only* burgers and fries, you'd be getting too little of what you need. Besides, you'd be getting too much fat (hamburgers are fatty, fries are cooked in fat).

## Food Facts for Kids

In a nutshell, here are the three most important rules of nutrition for you:

1. DON'T eat too much sugar (all that candy!).
2. DON'T eat too much fat (all those burgers and fries!).
3. DO eat a variety of foods (a little of this, a little of that).

# Parents

See ARGUMENTS, EMERGENCIES, PRIVACY, and WORKING PARENTS.

# ✍ PARTIES ✍

## Planned Partyhood

Great parties don't just happen, they're planned. So before you put up a single piece of crepe paper, even before you send out a single invitation, you should do a little serious thinking. Some people find the planning part to be fun in itself: the anticipation of the party is a little like waiting for Christmas.

First of all, why are you having this party? Is it for someone's birthday (yours, perhaps)? To introduce a new kid at school to your other friends? Because it's Halloween? Because it's the third Friday after Groundhog Day? We're asking, because the "why" of the party makes a difference in the "how." If it's a birthday party, you'll probably want a cake; if it's to get new people together, you'll want to have lots of good party games ready; if it's Halloween, you may want to turn it into a costume party. (If it's the third Friday after Groundhog Day, you're on your own, kid.)

A theme party is fun for almost any occasion. Ask everyone to come as their favorite star. Or as a star — or anything else — from outer space. (This is known as a spaced-out party.) Slumber parties are good, too. It all depends on your friends, what you think they would enjoy most. If you're all into dancing, and you're going to have boys and girls, build the party around music. Picnics, barbecues, and pool parties are wonderful, but that means the weather has to be good. And you do need a pool for a pool party.

If you don't have a pool, but you do have enough money saved (or a parent who can afford to pick up the bill), give a skating party. Everyone meets at the rink, and, well . . . they skate.

## Short on Cash . . .

Which brings us to a very important point: money. You may have the greatest ideas in the world, but not much cash. If that's the case, but you and your parents want you to have this party, keep it simple, short, and sweet. Bake a big cake (or two), or lots of cookies, save up enough

money from your allowance or job to get enough ice cream and milk to go around, gather lots of records or games to play, invite the gang over after school, and that's that. Nothing wrong with that, either. You could also organize a party with a group of people, so that you all contribute something, and no one person spends a lot of money.

## . . . But Long on "Dash"!

It's possible to have a really special party with very little money, but that takes imagination. How about a scavenger hunt? You know how this works: you

make up lists of silly, hard-to-find things, and divide the guests up into teams. Your house is just the base for the party, so you don't need a lot of food or fancy decorations. You could bake up some of our famous fudge brownies (recipe on page 77), and have them ready to serve with milk as the teams come back with their treasures. The real fun is the hunt, not the food.

Remember, you don't have to be a copycat when it comes to parties. If the most popular kid at school had a slumber party, you can too. But you don't have to. If you come up with a different idea — one that you feel comfortable with — then your party can be a success, too.

## Get Organized

The fastest and easiest way we know to organize your party is to make three (count 'em: three) lists:

List #1: Who to Invite
List #2: What to Get
List #3: What to Do

### LIST #1: WHO TO INVITE

Even though you don't want to hurt anyone's feelings, you can't invite everyone at school. Think about these things when you're making your guest list:

- How much space you have for the party
- How much money you can spend
- How the people get along (they don't all have to be best friends, but if even a few are known enemies, there could be trouble)
- Whose parties you have been invited to
- Whether you'll be having boys and girls (if so, make the number of each about even)

Once you've made the list, send out invitations with all the necessary information on them, with RSVP written on the bottom, so people will tell you if they're coming or not. You could also call the guests by phone and tell them all about it: time, place, kind of party.

### LIST #2: WHAT TO GET

First of all, there's food. Here are some

ideas, but your own tastes and budget will help you make the final decisions:

- Sandwiches, cut into quarters so they're easy to handle
- Big hero sandwiches, cut into slices
- Cookies, cakes, cupcakes
- Chips, pretzels, popcorn, crackers (with dips), peanuts, pizza
- Raw vegetables and dip — only if you know your guests will like this, or if they're all on a diet!

Then, something to drink:

- Homemade lemonade (recipe on page 77)
- Punch (make your own by mixing a variety of fruit juices)
- Cider (icy cold in summer; hot in winter, with cinnamon sticks)
- Colas, club soda, hot chocolate, milk (to go with cookies or cake)

Plus, things to eat and drink with (some of which you may already have at home):

- Paper plates
- Plastic forks, spoons, knives, cups
- Napkins

And decorations, if you want them:

- Paper table coverings
- Streamers, balloons

Anything *special* you need for your particular party, such as:

- A birthday cake
- Prizes for games
- Party favors
- Scavenger lists (if it's a hunt)
- Towels (if it's a pool party)

## LIST #3: WHAT TO DO (BESIDES MAKING ALL THESE LISTS)

Try to get everything done well before the time of the party, so that you can get yourself ready.

- A day or so before, do some checking to find out that all the people who said they're coming really are, so that there won't be any surprises (unless it's a surprise party).
- Also check to make sure that anyone who promised to bring something — food, records, decorations — is really going to do it.
- Plan your music: a radio is fine, but if you're using records, have them cleaned and in one place, ready to play.
- Rearrange the furniture, roll up the rug, or make any other preparations *before* the guests arrive.

## Party Time!

The great thing about all this planning in advance is that once the party gets going, you can enjoy it along with your guests. Try to talk to everyone (not all at once, unless you want to make a speech), to make them all feel at home. And try to get everyone talking to everyone else (again, not at once, unless you want to have a shouting match). This is called mingling. It's also called having a good party.

If something should go wrong, like someone spilling the punch, just clean it up, and — carry on!

## Going to a Party

What's to say about being a guest? You go to a party, that's that. Not quite. The best guest — who is more likely to get invited to more parties — knows about some or all of these things:

• Let the person who's giving the party know you're coming.

• Be on time, especially if you've promised to help.

• Ask if you can help, but don't make a big deal out of it. (You could make the person feel like a klutz who can't take care of it alone.)

• Eat and drink. (Work has gone into preparing all that stuff, and the party giver feels bad if it just sits there.)

• But don't make a pig out of yourself. (There are other mouths to feed.)

• Be careful with other people's property.

• If you do break or spill something, help clean it up.

• Don't just sit there — mingle!

• Have a good time.

## PET CARE

### The Best Pet

Almost everyone loves pets. And almost no one loves taking care of them. That's why there are so many arguments in families about pets: you wanted that puppy — you begged for it, even — and now that he's a full-grown dog (with big needs), you don't always look after him. Sound familiar? It's the same with cats, and birds, and fish, and you-name-it.

Once it's yours, it's yours to take care of, too.

So if you have any choice in which pet your family gets, think about what you'll have to do to make that animal happy and healthy. Dogs take a lot of care, then come cats, then animals like rabbits, hamsters, guinea pigs, and turtles, and birds and fish. If you don't want to work at all, get a pet rock!

## Chow Time

But even if you didn't choose your family's pet, you still may have the job of feeding it. Every pet should be fed on a schedule: about the same time and same amount every day. Of course, this depends on the pet: you wouldn't feed a Saint Bernard the way you would a canary. You'll find out what your pet's diet is from your parent, the pet store, the vet, or all of the above. And no matter what the diet is, fresh water should *always* be there.

If your pet won't eat, don't try to force him. Tell your parent. Very often, not wanting to eat is a sign of illness in animals, and your pet may have to see a vet.

## Cleanup Time

*Dogs:* Okay, your dog is (finally!) housebroken, so you don't usually have to clean up after him. But once in a while, bless his

little heart, he has an "accident." The first thing you do is take him to the spot, point to the mess, and scold him. No need to get really nasty, he just needs a reminder that this is not the thing to do. (Especially on the living room carpet. When you're having company. And it's your father's or mother's boss.)

Clean up the mess, with newspapers or paper towels, then wash the area with a sponge or rag dampened in warm soapy water. Rub well. Keep doing this until the stain (and the smell) is gone. Then rinse with a damp sponge and clear water, and let it dry.

*Cats:* They take care of themselves pretty well, but they do use litter boxes, and the litter has to be changed. Don't wait until the smell is so bad that it knocks you off your feet when you come into the house: clean it often.

Throw out the dirty litter in the garbage. *Do not flush it down the toilet!* That can cause all kinds of plumbing problems. Wash out the box with soap and water, rinse it well, and dry it. The floor under and around the box usually collects some litter, so clean it, too. Put fresh litter in the box and, if you have some, mix in about one cup of baking soda. This helps keep the litter smelling sweet.

If the litter is not very dirty or smelly, but does have solid pieces of waste in it, get this out with a litter sifter or scooper. It's okay to flush this (*but not the litter!*) down the toilet.

It's a good idea to have a scratching post for your cat. The idea is for the cat to scratch it — and not the furniture! — to its heart's content.

*Fish:* Tanks have to be cleaned regularly, too. But how and how often depends on the kind of fish you have. It's best to

have your parent give you a demonstration before you try it yourself. Again, pet stores are usually very helpful with this kind of information.

*Pets in Cages:* A person's home may be his castle, but a pet's home is often his cage. The first step in cleaning a cage is usually to remove the animal and put him in a safe place, such as a pet carrier or a box (with tiny holes for air punched in it, and tape to keep it closed). Take out the dirty shavings or paper, and throw it in the garbage. Then wash the cage, and the food and water dishes. Rinse and dry

everything completely, so your pet's cage won't be as damp as a real castle. Give the cage fresh shavings or paper. Then put in

food and water, and other things like toys or chewing sticks. And before you close the cage, don't forget to put in the most important thing of all: the pet!

## Walking the Dog

No, this isn't a yo-yo trick, it's one of the things you have to do, every day, for a dog. (We told you dogs take a great deal of care.) The first and most important rule of dog walking is: *always use a leash!* Even if your beloved pooch is well trained and obedient (which is more than you can say for most of your friends), a dog can get into trouble if he's allowed to roam free.

The leash is for his safety. So if you love him, use it. Hold on to the leash tightly at all times. And if your dog tends to fight with other dogs, stay away from places where neighborhood dog walkers go.

On city streets, stay as close to the curb as possible so your dog can do it in the street, but out of the way of traffic. It's a good idea — and in some cities, it's the law — to clean up after your dog with a newspaper or pooper scooper.

Walking the dog doesn't just give him the chance to take care of business, it also gives him exercise. So walk him around for a while; the exercise is good for you, too.

## Washing the Dog

If this is one of your jobs, try to do it on a warm day in your backyard. And this job can get pretty messy, so it's not the time to wear your best clothes.

Use special dog shampoo or tearless baby shampoo, and have a wet cloth handy for the pooch's face, ears, and muzzle. Use a hose to get the suds off, but don't get water in his ears.

Small dogs can usually be washed in the bathtub. If you do wash him there, be sure to keep him confined in the bathroom immediately afterward, and watch out: your dog will try to shake off his bath.

▶ NOTES:

# ❧ PHONE CALLS ❧

## Hang Up Your Hangups

Some people get so confused on the phone they'll mutter, stutter, and sputter. Don't let this happen to you! Pick up that phone and show it who's boss! Just don't pick it up too often, or you'll have gigantic phone bills and angry parents to be afraid of.

## For Safety's Sake

Avoid answering the phone by saying "Smith residence," or anything else that tells your name. Saying "Hello" is enough. Never give your phone number (it could have been dialed by chance),

your name, address, or other information when you don't know the caller. And don't say that you're home alone or babysitting.

## Getting the Message

When you answer the phone and the call is not for you (it can't *always* be), and the person the call is for isn't home, ask for the name of the caller and the message. And, since nobody can remember everything, don't take chances: write down the message right away. Keep a pad and pen or pencil handy near the phone and leave the message there, or in a place where the person who's supposed to get it will see it.

## A Short Report on Long Distance

*Rates:* Of course, you've checked with a parent before you call Cousin Mortimer in Honolulu. It does cost quite a bit more than phoning your friend down the block. But there are different rates for long distance depending on the day and time. The cheapest rates are any day after 11:00 P.M. If that's too late, find out the costs for calling after 5:00 P.M. or on weekends. Dial direct, if you can: it's less expensive, and before you make a long-distance call to a business, check to see whether there's an "800" toll-free number you can use.

*Collect calls:* If you've been instructed to call someone collect, so that the other person will pay for the call, here's what you do: dial or press "O" for Operator, then the area code, then the number. When the phone rings, the operator will come on the line, and you should say, "This is a collect call from ——— (your name here)." You may hear the phone ring again, but when the person answers, let the operator speak first. The person has to agree to accept the charges before you can talk.

*Person-to-person:* Sometimes you want to speak to one person, and that person only, and you're not sure they'll be in when you call. Again, dial or press "O," the area code and number, then speak to the operator: "This is a person-to-person call to ——— (whomever you want to talk to)." If the person isn't there, you can leave your name and number and when you can be reached. But you can't give any other messages, or you'll be charged for the call.

You can also make a person-to-person call collect. Tell the operator, "This is a collect, person-to-person call from ——— to ———." Then wait for that person to answer and accept the charges.

*Away from home:* You can bill a call to your home number if you have to make a long-distance call from a phone other than your own — from a friend's house or a pay phone. Dial "O," the area code and number, then tell the operator you want to bill the call to your number. The operator will take your name and number, and

will sometimes call your home to make sure it's okay to make the call.

Remember, all these special kinds of calls are expensive, so don't make them unless you've got permission or it's an emergency.

## Your Rights

When you get a wrong number, a poor connection, or are cut off, hang up and dial the operator and tell her/him. If you're calling from a pay phone, you'll get a refund (usually via mail); if you're calling from home, you won't be charged for the call. If you keep dialing a number

that you're sure is correct and it doesn't ring, dial the operator and ask for help.

## Out of Order

No dial tone? It could be very temporary, so hang up and wait awhile. If the line is still dead after about ten minutes, go to a neighbor's home and call the phone company. (If that line is out, too, then it's probably a neighborhood problem and you'll have to wait it out.) The phone company has a twenty-four-hour repair service, and its number is listed in the front of your local phone directory. Tell your parents about the trouble on the line even if it's fixed by the time they're home.

## Emergency Calls

To help you stay calm in an emergency, have a list of emergency numbers in view by the phone so you won't have to tear up the house searching for them. You should also fill in the list on the last page of this book and keep it handy. Then all you have to do is:

1. Call the right number. (When in doubt, call *police*.)

2. State your problem as simply as possible. (Say, "My house is on fire!" Don't say, "Hey, I'm in trouble, and there's smoke, and I think I need a fire engine.")

3. State your name and where you are. (Speak clearly.)

4. Don't hang up until you're told to. (The person may need more directions, or want to give you special instructions.)

5. Go out to the road to "signal" the help that's coming. (If you can't go, send someone else.)

## Cranks and Pranks

Not everyone in the world is like you: kind, considerate, intelligent, wonderful. There are some people out there who are Grade-A nut cases! And some of them like to spend their time making other people miserable via the phone.

Sometimes, when you're home alone, the phone rings and no one answers when you pick it up. If this happens once, forget it. Someone may just have the wrong number, or there's trouble with the connection. But if it happens many times in a row, it is probably being done on purpose. What should you do? Not much — but a lot. Just hang up. That's it. Don't ask who it is, don't act angry or scared, don't make threats, and don't keep saying "Hello." All that does is encourage the person making the call. But if you just quietly hang up, you show that you're calm and in control. Almost always, the person will give up.

But what if the calls keep coming, or if the person says anything crazy or obscene? Again, hang up *immediately*. Then call the Annoyance Call Bureau at the telephone company.

The person making these kinds of calls can be anyone — even a classmate trying to tease you. So don't tell everyone about it or show that it upset you. If you act as if nothing happened, and the caller is someone who knows you, they'll probably get bored and think you're "no fun." So much the better for you.

On the other hand, *always* tell your par-

ents about any of these calls. (If you're babysitting, tell your employer.) It might just be from a silly prankster, but it might be from someone with a serious problem.

## It's Not Cool to Be a "Crank"

We know what you're thinking. You probably have made at least one silly call

yourself. Well, don't feel too guilty. Almost everyone has. You do it to be funny, or to get even with someone, or because you're bored. Or sometimes, you've dialed the wrong number by mistake, and don't bother to answer when you hear a strange voice at the other end. Now that you know how scary crank calls can be, you probably won't be tempted to do that in the future.

◆ NOTES:

_____
_____
_____
_____
_____

# Planes

See PUBLIC TRANSPORTATION.

## PLANT CARE

### The Way to Water

If the family plants are left in your care, this usually means simply watering them from time to time. Easy? Yes and no. It's certainly easy to water a plant — just pour it in, gently. The question is: how much and how often? Get very careful directions from your parents because underwatering — and especially overwatering — can kill a houseplant. And you're too young to be a murderer!

### Hanging Around with Plants

Perhaps you want plants of your own, to hang (or sit) around your room, keep you company, and give you nicer air to breathe. In that case, you'll have to learn more than just watering. You have to find out how much sunlight each plant needs — every one is different — so you'll know where to put it. You may have to mist them with water, or add fertilizer or plant food to the soil. You may even have to trim them or transplant them to bigger pots when they grow up, or start new plants with the cuttings from the old ones.

If you're still interested in growing greenery, now that you know it's not that simple, get directions from anyone with a "green thumb": your local florist, your mom or dad, your grandmother, your

PLANT CARE · 183

Great Aunt Clara. And be prepared for a few failures until you get the hang of it.

What about talking to plants? Well, what about it! Many people believe it really helps. And it certainly can't hurt. Just don't say anything *nasty* to your green things. They may be very sensitive.

◆ NOTES:

_____

_____

_____

_____

_____

  POISONING

## There's Poison All around You!

We're not talking about murder-mystery-type poison, where the villain puts a few drops of rare tropical liquid into the unsuspecting victim's nice cup of tea, and *arrgh!* he keels over, stiff as a board. We're talking about accidently swallowing something — like cleaning fluid or bleach — which acts as a poison. So, whenever you see these warnings on a label

☠ | *Not for Internal Use* | or | *Caution* | ☠

you can be pretty sure that whatever's inside will poison you if you take it internally (swallow it).

*YOU* can read. But can your little brother? Or the twins you're babysitting for? Even adults who ought to know better sometimes drink poison by accident. And medicines, which can cure an illness in one person, can have a poisonous effect on someone else. (That's one of the reasons that you get prescriptions with *your name* on them.)

## Poison Control

If someone is poisoned, here's what you do:

**1. CALL THE POISON CONTROL CENTER (OR YOUR DOCTOR) — FAST!** These numbers should be near your phone. (See *Emergency Calls,* page 181.)

**2. Find the poison and read the label.** Some bottles have emergency instructions or antidotes printed on the labels. You also can use the bottle to describe the poison to the doctor.

**3. Unless the label says otherwise, give the person as much warm water as he can swallow.** This helps to dilute the poison in the body.

## What about Vomiting?

Should you make the person throw up to get rid of the poison? **Only if the doctor tells you to.** Some poisons, like drain cleaners, do more harm when they're vomited.

If you're told to induce vomiting, follow these steps:

1. Give one tablespoon of ipecac syrup, if you have it. If not, tickle the back of the throat with a spoon handle.

2. Give the person as much warm water as he will drink.

3. Hold his/her head down over the sink basin until vomiting is finished.

4. If vomiting doesn't take place within fifteen minutes, give one more tablespoon of ipecac syrup, and one more glass of water.

*Don't* give a salt solution to induce vomiting.

Save clean-up for later. The doctor may be able to identify the kind of poison by the vomitus left in the sink.

**If the person is unconscious, call for an ambulance fast!** If there's vomitus, bring some to the doctor.

As you sit there, calmly reading a book, all this may sound really revolting. But, remember, in an emergency you won't be thinking about how things look or smell. You'll want to do your best to save the situation — and maybe someone's life.

See also FIRST AID, and ACCIDENT PREVENTION, for some tips on preventing poisoning.

◆ NOTES:

_____

_____

_____

_____

_____

# Power Failure

See BLACKOUTS and ELECTRICAL PROBLEMS.

# ❧ PRIVACY ❧

## Yours...

The friendliest, most outgoing person in the world sometimes needs to be alone. But if you have a large family or a small home, that can be difficult. How can you have any privacy when you share a room with brothers or sisters?

If that's your problem talk it over with your parents. They probably value their own privacy and will understand your complaint. Maybe you can work something out with their help. Such as? Well, you could ask to use their room for an hour or so after school or on certain evenings when they're out or watching TV in the living room. Or you could arrange it that certain times when friends visit, you could

have the use of your room with no (repeat: NO) interruptions from your brother or sister.

## ...and Theirs

Respecting other people's privacy is a good way to encourage them to respect yours. If the door to your parents' room is closed, and you want to go in, knock first. If your older sister is having a "private" phone conversation, don't listen in. Resist the temptation to read anyone else's mail, even if it is lying there on the table. If you do these things, you're inviting people to do the same to you.

See also BROTHERS AND SISTERS.

# ⁍ PUBLIC TRANSPORTATION ⁌

## Moving Right — Alone

There's nothing mysterious about using public transportation — buses, trains, trams, or trolleys — but it can be confusing the first few times. So before you set out on your own — crosstown or cross country — face a few facts for travelers:

🚂 🚂 🚂

• Know the *exact* name of the stop you're going to. On a train, it might be something like "Yorktown Junction" (which could be a different stop from *"East* Yorktown *Heights"*). Pay attention. On a bus, it's probably just a street: you're riding along Third Avenue, and you want to go to 56th Street, and the nearest stop is 57th Street, so that's what you're looking for. It could also be the name of a landmark, such as Union Square or Elm Street Park.

• Find out what the stop *before* your stop is, so you'll be ready. Your folks or friends may know. But the safest way is to ask the bus driver, train conductor, or ticket taker.

🐫 🐫 🐫

• If you're still afraid you might miss your stop (you shouldn't sleep on buses or trains, but it could happen), take a seat up front by the bus driver, or ask the conductor or ticket taker to remind you when your stop comes up.

• For long trips, check the schedules carefully and get there *on time*.

• For short rides, find out how often your bus or train runs. It's sometimes posted on subway stations, and you can get written schedules at train stations, bus terminals, or sometimes from the bus driver.

• If you're leaving from a big terminal or station, make sure you know the bus or train line you're riding on. If possible, find out the gate number before you get there.

• If your final destination (even on a short trip) is a big station, it's best to be met by someone who knows the area. The crowds and congestion can make you feel rattled.

🐎 🐎 🐎

• If you have to do it alone, then follow the signs, and ask questions. Whom to ask: conductors, transit officials, police officers. Whom not to ask: strangers. They may not know the correct information, and you may be asking for trouble.

⛵ ⛵ ⛵

• Be sure to have enough money for the fare, plus a little extra — at least enough for a phone call or two. For a long trip, have cash for meals or snacks, too.

• On long trips, it's also a good idea to have something to read, such as (guess what?) *The Official Kids' Survival Kit*. Take it along, and see how far it gets you.

## Subway Safety

Some subway systems publish booklets with safety tips. Such as:

- Don't stand at the end of an empty platform, or too close to the edge of a platform.
- Ride the center car, near the conductor, whenever possible.
- Travel with a friend, whenever possible.
- Don't walk between the cars when the train is moving.
- Never go on the tracks — for *any* reason.

## Don't Tempt a Thief

On any kind of public transportation, you shouldn't invite trouble by showing off anything valuable, such as money. What money? Well, even if you aren't carrying hundreds of dollars, don't flash a bunch of dollar bills (a thief could think they were hundreds, not singles). And if you carry a purse or camera, don't swing it around or hold it so it could easily be grabbed. (See also the section on SAFETY AND SECURITY.)

## The Plane Facts

Plane travel is a little different from any other means of public transportation. It's usually a special occasion, and it's more complicated — with all those reservations, and tickets, and getting to the airport, and getting your baggage checked, and picking a seat, and all the other airport procedures. You'll no doubt have help with most of that, but once you're on the plane, you're on your own. Well, not really. The flight attendants are there to take care of you, and they usually do an excellent job.

Without overdoing it, ask questions about anything that's bothering you: when you're going to get something to eat, why the engine is making that funny noise, why the lights in the john don't go on, and what does *ocupado* mean, anyway? (That there's someone in there.) A flight attendant or other airline representative can even help you get your baggage and find the people you're supposed to be meeting, if you want them to.

Don't ever be embarrassed to ask for help: it's their job, and the last thing they want is an ODC (Official Dissatisfied Customer).

 Through

You've heard it all before: never hitchhike or get into a stranger's car, never accept gifts from someone you don't know, etc., etc., etc. But it is true. Sometimes, being safe and secure means avoiding danger by being alert and sensible. The purpose of this section is to make you aware of dangerous situations and to give you information on how to help yourself if you have to.

## Safe at Home

Be on the safe side when you're at home by keeping the following suggestions in mind.

### LOCK UP
When you are home, *always keep the door locked!* And if you should leave your house — even for a minute — *lock the door.* And lock it again when you get back. Remember: even the best lock in the world is useless if it remains unlocked. And never, never, *never* leave your keys in the door, not even if the phone's ringing and you're in a rush to answer it, not even if you're just going to take the garbage out.

### LIGHTS ON
Lights inside and outside of doorways are terrific protection. Leave them on at night, even if you're going out for a short time. When you come home, have your keys ready. With a light on, you won't have to fumble for your keys, and if someone unexpected is there, you'll be able to see him.

### SOMEONE'S AT THE DOOR
If you're home alone and someone comes to the door whom you don't know, *don't let the person in!* Make *no* exceptions, no matter what he says, even if he claims to be the police. If you're expecting a delivery, see the section on DELIVERIES; otherwise, follow this procedure — *with the door locked:*

- Ask the person to identify himself. If he claims to be a repairman or a building inspector, tell him to come back later (give him a time when you *know* an adult will be home).

- If someone says they have to deliver a telegram and they need your signature, have them slip the paper under the door and leave the telegram outside the door.

- If someone tells you it's an emergency — her car broke down, there was an accident — and she *must* use your phone,

tell her you'll make the call for her. (If the emergency is a real one, there's probably little more than that you can do for her, anyway.)

- If you're babysitting, don't let the visitor know it. Just say that the parents "aren't available right now," and politely ask that he/she come back another time. Even if it's a neighbor who wants to borrow a cup of sugar, don't let him/her in if you don't know the person. Remember, the parents have trusted you with their children and won't mind if you're overcautious.

- If the person won't go away, keeps knocking, or returns from time to time, tell him you're going to call the police — and do it.

*SOMEONE'S TRYING TO BREAK IN*
When you're home alone or babysitting and you see someone suspicious prowling around the house, or you think someone is trying to break into the house, *call the police*

*immediately* and give them detailed information. Lock yourself (and the children) in a bedroom with a phone in it. If there's no way to lock the door, prop a chair under the doorknob (you might even do this if the door locks).

## Safe Away from Home

First of all, here are two general tips:

- On your way home, *never* flash your keys around so that everyone can see you're going to let yourself in (a sure sign that no one but you is likely to be home!). Keep your keys in a place where you can reach them easily.

- Always have some extra change with you. If you have to make an emergency call from a pay phone, or if it would be better to take a bus rather than walk, you'll have the money to do so.

*TRAVELING*
If it's late at night, and you have a choice, take a bus rather than a train. And try to

sit up front, within the bus driver's view. That way, you can ask the driver for help if someone is bothering you. If you have to take a subway or train, choose a car with lots of people. (See PUBLIC TRANSPORTATION for more about this.)

While it's always best to travel with a friend, if you must walk alone (especially at night), stick to the streets you know and walk close to the curb. Stay away from dark streets with little traffic. And avoid shortcuts that take you into parks, wooded areas, dark alleys, deserted lots, and unfamiliar places.

## BEING FOLLOWED

You're on your way home. You haven't taken a shortcut or flashed your keys around, but you think someone is following you by foot or by car. What can you

do? Don't tell yourself that you've been watching too many detective shows and just let the person keep following you. Act on your instincts, which are often right. Try this:

- Go up to someone on the street, or go into a nearby store or restaurant.
- If that doesn't work, change your direction, or try to hail a taxi. (Don't worry about not having enough money to pay for it. When you get home, ask your parents or a neighbor for the fare.)
- If you're really scared and no one's around, scream and run as fast as you can.
- If you're close to home, *don't* go into your house if you know no one is home. Go to a neighbor's house (someone you *know* will be home) and explain what's happening.

## STRANGERS IN ELEVATORS

If you're waiting for a self-service elevator with someone who makes you feel uncomfortable, or with someone you think might have followed you, let the person get on the elevator alone. If you see the person is waiting for you to get on, make a casual comment ("Whoops, forgot the mail . . ."), and walk toward the doorman or guard (if there is one) or simply leave the building — fast.

If you're already on the elevator with someone who makes you nervous, get off at the very next floor. Then go to a neighbor's apartment on that floor. Tell your neighbor about your concern and ask him or her to escort you home — to your door. If no one is there to help you, go back to the lobby and, if no one's there, leave the building.

## *TRUST YOUR INSTINCTS*

If you notice something is wrong when you get home — the door is slightly ajar, the lock looks broken, a window that's usually closed is open or broken — *don't go inside!* Someone may be in there. Instead, go to a pay phone or a neighbor's house and call your parents. Let them know what happened. *Don't* go home until your parents or the police get there. Sure, it may only be your big brother returning home unexpectedly, but it could be someone who has entered your home illegally. Stay away and let adults do the investigating.

### A
### SPECIAL NOTE

Reading all this stuff about security — locking doors, being followed, break-ins — may make you a bit nervous. Don't be frightened by every sound you hear or every stranger you meet. Just be aware of real dangers and take precautions to avoid problems. And when you're home alone or babysitting, don't scare yourself by watching horror movies or reading mystery books. This is no time for *The Case of the Incredible Squeaking Closet.*

See also KEYS — LOST and PHONE CALLS.

◆ NOTES:

_____
_____
_____
_____
_____

## ✍ SCHOOLWORK ✍

### Do It — and It's Done

If you ignore some things, they just go away. Schoolwork is *not* one of these things. If you tend to put things off, remind yourself that it's there, it has to be done, and once you've finished, you can stop thinking about it and get on to something else. Besides, once you've tackled it, it usually isn't as bad as you thought, and you get a good feeling from being on top of the situation. Many kids even enjoy it and/or actually learn something.

Even if you have chores to do, or team practice to attend, or music lessons to take, or whatever, set aside a certain time to do your school assignments. If you find, after doing all this, that you have no time left over for yourself, talk to your parents about it. It may be that you're doing too much — and something's got to go!

## Problems with the Problems

Or it may be that you're having trouble with your schoolwork and it's taking too long. (Maybe that's why you put off doing it.) If you are having trouble, speak up. It doesn't mean that you're stupid, it's simply that you're having a problem. If it happens to be with those arithmetic problems you just can't understand, listen to this: Einstein, the famous mathematical genius, used to do very poorly in arithmetic when he was in grade school. It's true! There's hope for anyone to do better — unless you sit there and don't tell anyone what's going on.

If you need help, talk to your teacher about it first. Then try to follow his/her suggestions. Suppose you're told to get help from your parents. Fine. But don't

expect your mom or dad to drop everything, anytime you say, to work with you. And don't call your parents at work with a schoolwork problem unless they've told you to. Ask an older brother or sister to help. Or check with a classmate who's

good at that subject. You may simply have to wait until your parents get home. Which is another good reason to have a schedule worked out for doing your school assignments at a time when your parents are available for help.

Suppose you're doing fine in school, but you just can't figure out the assignment you're supposed to do tonight. Not only that, but your parents don't understand it either, *and* you've tried to reach a classmate, with no luck, *and* you've even called your smart Uncle Norman who knows *everything,* and he's out of town. What are you supposed to do now? Just do your best. Then talk it over with your teacher the first chance you get the next day. The best way to avoid a misunderstanding is for you to ask about it before he/she asks you. That way, it will be known that you honestly tried to do the work. Unless this happens too often — like every day — your teacher will probably be quite understanding. (If you don't get along with your teacher, talk to your grade adviser or guidance counselor.)

## SCRATCHES

"It's just a scratch" is something you'll hear (and say) about as often as "He started it!" Nothing to get excited about, just treat it like a cut: clean it with warm, soapy water. See the section on CUTS AND SCRAPES. If the scratch was caused by an animal, you may want to have the animal checked out by a vet. See BITES.

◆ NOTES:

_____

_____

_____

_____

_____

There's one problem that many kids have had, but usually weren't encouraged to talk about. Sometimes, adults pay more attention to you, in a physical way, than you feel comfortable about. It can be

really awkward if the person is someone you and your parents know and trust: like a relative, a friend of the family, someone you babysit for, even a teacher.

In the past, you weren't supposed to say too much, because "nice people" just didn't do this kind of thing. So if it hap-

pened to you, then somehow *you* must have caused it. *Not true!* Practically no one believes that anymore. Still, it can be embarrassing to admit that a friend's mother or father (or other adult) has made sexual advances to you.

The "advances" don't even have to be physical to be disturbing. If an adult begins talking to you in a sexual way, and you don't like it, then you're being put in a bad situation.

The point is that you *shouldn't feel guilty,* and you shouldn't keep it to yourself. First of all, tell the person that you object. You don't have to get uptight: just quietly let it be known that you don't like being treated like that. You may be smaller than an adult, but you're not a toy for anyone to play with.

If at all possible, tell one of your parents. If you can't bring yourself to do this, at least discuss it with someone older, not a friend your own age. (A friend's parent can be a good choice.) You may want to tell a friend, but an adult is more likely to be able to help. And talking about it with an older person may make it easier to bring it up with your parent.

Sometimes, the person is someone in your immediate family, and this makes it even worse. Be sure to discuss it with an

adult you really trust. Remember, the person who is making these advances needs help, too.

*A word of warning:* Don't become super suspicious. An adult who's being friendly may be just that: an adult who's being friendly. A person who puts his/her arm around you probably just wants to be your friend, and you're lucky to have one in an older person. But you can sense when it's more than just friendliness. And that's the time to complain.

## ❧ SHOCK ❧

### What It Is

You know what "shock" usually means: to greatly surprise or offend. And there's another kind of "shock" that is caused by electricity (see ELECTRICAL SHOCK). But "shock" is also a medical term. It's what may happen when a person has a serious injury or a sudden illness. Technically, shock takes place when there is not enough blood circulating in the right parts of the body.

### What It Looks Like

So what does the body do? On the inside, it's reacting in complicated ways. On the outside, it shows these kinds of symptoms:

- **Pale face and dull, vacant eyes**
- **Cold, clammy skin**
- **Nausea (and sometimes vomiting)**
- **Weakness, trembling, nervousness, or unconsciousness**
- **Irregular, shallow, or rapid breathing**
- **Weak, but rapid, pulse**

### What to Do

The two basic steps are:

**1. Have the person lie down and remain quiet.**
**2. Get medical help — immediately!**

### What to Do until Help Arrives

If you see that the person is having trouble breathing, try propping a pillow under his or her shoulders. If the breathing is all right — and *only* if it is — then raise the feet about a foot off the ground, so that the person is lying on a slant. This helps the flow of blood to the brain.

See also FIRST AID.

♦ NOTES:

## Shoes/Sneakers

See CLOTHING CARE.

## Shopping

See FOOD SHOPPING and MONEY.

## Sisters

See BROTHERS AND SISTERS.

## Skin Problems

See ACNE.

☞

## ∿ SMOKE ∿

### Where There's Smoke . . .

**If you see or smell a lot of smoke, chances are there's a fire. Stay calm and get out fast.**

If there's only a faint smell of smoke, try to find the source: maybe something is burning on the stove or in the oven, maybe someone's cigarette has dropped on the carpet. If you can find the source of the smoke, try to extinguish it. If not, or if the smell of smoke gets stronger, alert everyone and get out fast.

See also FIRE.

◆ NOTES:

_____

_____

_____

_____

_____

_____

## ⚜ SMOKING ⚜

*An Official Survival Tip:* **Don't start.** If you want it from another official source, the Surgeon General of the United States has determined that cigarette smoking is dangerous to your health.

If your parents smoke, there's really not much you can do to stop them. They're already aware of the dangers. The best you can do is express your concern — not twelve times a day — once or twice is enough. Who knows, one day one of your

parents might say, "What can I do to get you to stop eating all that junk?" And you might make them an offer they (probably) can't refuse: *quit smoking.*

## Snacks

See COOKING.

# SPILLS

Don't cry over spilt milk — just wipe it up right away. That's true for anything you spill, because the longer it sits, the more it sets. Then it will be harder to clean up, and might leave a stain. Soak up as much of the spill as possible with paper towels or sponges, then rinse with clear water.

With greasy stuff, such as butter, oil, or gravy, be sure that it's not only wiped up, but that the place you spilled it on is grease-free. (When characters in a cartoon fall on a slippery surface, it's funny. In real life, it isn't.) Use soap and water, then rinse with clear water. If that doesn't do the job, sprinkle lightly with powder (such

as talcum or cornstarch), then rinse and wipe again.

See also STAINS and BROKEN DISHES/ GLASS, if necessary.

# SPLINTERS

Splinters are tiny little things. No big deal — except when you get one. You'll definitely live, but you'll probably feel rotten until it's out.

## Good-bye, Splinter!

Unless you're dealing with a major splinter, which should be removed by a doctor, here's what you do:

1. Wash the area with warm water and soap. (Soapsuds help to soften the skin around the splinter and make it easier to get out.)

2. Sterilize a tweezer or needle with rubbing alcohol. (You can also sterilize it by passing it through a flame a few times. Be very careful about fire if you use this method.)

3. Use the tweezer or needle to take out the splinter. Be as gentle as you can.

4. After it's out, press the area softly to make it bleed a little. (Even a few drops of blood will help clean out small bits of dirt that you can't even see.)

5. Wash again with warm water and soap, and dry.

6. It's a good idea to put a small bandage over the area.

One more thing: if possible, let a person remove his/her own splinter. Help only if you have to.

▶ NOTES:

_____

_____

_____

_____

## ✺ SPRAINS AND STRAINS ✺

The big question on people's minds about these kinds of injuries is whether to treat them with heat or cold. The answer is both, but in a very definite order.

### Cold Comfort

The first thing you do — as soon as possible after the injury — is to apply cold compresses or ice packs. It's a good idea to do this off and on for two to three hours. Why cold? When you get an injury like a sprained ankle or strained muscle, there's actual bleeding in the area. Your body tries to help by sending emergency blood supplies to the area that's hurt. The problem is that it sends too much blood and this causes swelling. When you put on the ice, the amount of bleeding will decrease, and the swelling will go down.

Even when you're not applying cold to the injury, whatever you do, *don't* put anything hot on it. Not for forty-eight to seventy-two hours. After that, you use heat to bring the blood back to the area, and help speed the healing process.

## Careful and Comfortable

You should also treat the person carefully and make him/her feel as comfortable as possible. Raise the injured part by propping it up with pillows, without moving it around too much. Call a doctor as soon as you can, tell him/her what you've done, and follow any special directions you get.

See also FIRST AID.

See also FIRST AID.

♦ NOTES:

_____

_____

_____

_____

_____

## ❧ STAINS ☙

### Whoops!

Chocolate - chip - fudge - nugget - chunky - cream pie is a wonderful thing. Except when you get it all over the front of your shirt, the top of the tablecloth, and in one big gloppy mess in the middle of the carpet. Before you consider leaving town, consider this: you can probably get rid of the stain (or most of it) if you ACT FAST. The longer a stain stays, the more likely it is to stay forever (something like your Aunt Henrietta from Cleveland).

There are many ways to take out a stain, and we're only going to tell you about the easiest ones. But one trick that can save you a lot of grief — no matter what method of stain-removing you choose — is to test it first. You use a small piece of the material that won't show

much, like a spot on the carpet under the couch, the underside hem on a tablecloth, or the bottom of your shirt (which you

probably tuck into your pants). The idea is to see if what you use to remove the stain will change the fabric — make it fade or look very different in some way. If that happens, you could be doing more harm than good. Try different methods, hoping to find one that works well for you.

## What Kind of Stain Are You, Anyhow?

Stains come in three mouth-watering varieties:

Greasy
Nongreasy
Combination

*Greasy* stains come from dropping things like french fries, gravy, butter, oil of any kind.

*Nongreasy* stains you may know and not love are from soft drinks, juice, ink, coffee, or tea.

*Combination* stains come from dropping two or more things at one time: the fries *and* the cola (can't take you *anyplace!*).

Let's take these little buggers one at a time.

### GREASY STAINS

Soap or detergent will remove most greasy stains on washable things. On a big thing, like a chair, rub soap or detergent into the stain, then rinse the area with water. On a

smaller thing, like a shirt, rub the stain with soap or detergent, then wash the whole thing. *Don't rub it in too much.* Just bend the material so that the soap or detergent can work its way into the stain. Hold the fabric in both hands and work the stained area back and forth between your thumbs. If it isn't easy to bend, or if it's wool and has to be treated gently, work the detergent into the stain with the round part of a spoon.

Wait a minute! What if the stain is greasy, all right, but the material isn't washable? You still use soap or detergent. But you use very little, and you dilute it with water. After you've worked the di-

luted detergent into the stain, you remove it with a sponge that's been dampened in cool water. *Careful:* don't use too much soap or detergent — it's hard to get out.

Good news! If you can get to a greasy stain before it dries, you can sometimes get rid of it quickly by sprinkling it with something powdery — like talcum powder, cornmeal, or cornstarch. As the powder absorbs the stain, brush or shake it off and sprinkle on fresh powder. The only problem (you *knew* there'd be a problem, didn't you?) is that you sometimes can't remove the powder from certain dark materials. So, instead of the stain, you now have a big blotch of white. Wonderful. This is

another reason for testing your stain-removing moves on a hidden spot before you do the real thing.

Absorbent cloth, paper, and sponges can sometimes work in the same way, especially on things that take a long time to really absorb a stain, such as upholstered furniture and deep-pile rugs.

### NONGREASY STAINS

The first thing to try is water. But you might have to use more than just a little dab. Some stains won't come out unless you soak them thirty minutes or longer — sometimes overnight. If you don't think this is working, use soap or detergent, as you would for a greasy stain. And if the stain really hangs in there, try bleach. But be sure to read the package for directions, and make sure it's safe for the material you're trying to de-stain.

### COMBINATION STAINS

If this kind of mess happens to something washable, treat it like a greasy stain, using soap or detergent. If the material isn't washable, treat it like a nongreasy stain, with cold water.

## What about Those Stain Removers They Advertise on Television?

Ready-made stain removers are fine — if you use the right one for the right stain.

Chances are, when you get a stain, you won't have a thousand and one varieties to choose from, so it's just a matter of figuring out if you've got one that will do the trick. If so, use it (following the directions, of course). If not, try one of the other ways.

And even though the stain removers on TV always positively absolutely never (perish the thought!) fail to remove the stain quick as a wink without a trace, Real Life doesn't always work that way. Sometimes, nothing works. Not soap. Not water. Not detergent. Not talcum powder.

Not even something like paint remover, whose main job is to remove paint! Don't despair. Even professional cleaners sometimes have to give up after they've given it their best shot.

◆ NOTES:

_____
_____
_____
_____
_____

## ❧ STEREOS AND SOUND EQUIPMENT ❧

Whether it's your own or the family's stereo, treat it with care. Since these systems can be quite sensitive, be sure to follow the manufacturer's and/or your parent's instructions very carefully.

### For the Record

Well-kept records last longer and sound better. To start with, play only clean, undamaged records. Before you play one, make sure it isn't warped or badly scratched, then wipe it with a special cloth or record cleaner to get rid of the dust. Handle with care: always hold the record by the edges, not the grooves. And afterward, put it back into its jacket, and store the jackets upright, away from radiators or other sources of heat that could warp them.

### Music to Their Ears?

Be considerate when you play the stereo, radio, TV or any other sound equipment. If your family or neighbors complain, you might want to get earphones for yourself. Or earplugs for everyone else! But don't overdo the volume even then, because a steady diet of loud sounds can actually hurt your hearing — permanently.

## STOMACHACHES

### Listen to Your Tummy

Most stomachaches aren't very serious. But they hurt! If you get one, listen to what your stomach is trying to tell you. Did you eat too much? Too fast? Then just rest for a while, quietly if you can manage it, and don't add any more fuel (food) to the fire. But if you've skipped lunch — and breakfast, too? — then the old tummy may be crying out for nourishment. Feed it. But don't go bananas — eat lightly and slowly, then relax.

When a stomachache is very bad or lasts more than an hour or two, let your parent know. Stomachaches together with fever can also be serious.

### Babysitting Bellyaches

If a child you're babysitting for complains of a stomachache, ask him/her the same things you would ask yourself. When was the last time you ate? What did you eat? How much? Then follow the same steps we talked about above. Never force a child to eat, though, even if you think he/she should. And if the child is very pale or feverish, contact the parents right away.

♦ NOTES:

_____
_____
_____
_____
_____

# Storing Food

See FOOD SHOPPING.

## STORMS

Suppose you're alone in the house, or babysitting at a neighbor's place, when a bad storm comes up. The wind whistles, the shutters shudder, and — *yipes!* — the lights go out. Here's what you're going to do:

- Quick! Before the storm gets worse! Take in the cat, and anything else you've left outside that you wouldn't want to get soaking wet (or blown away).
- Don't go out, though, if the storm is really bad, unless there's an emergency. It's dangerous to be caught in a storm, especially a hurricane or tornado with high winds.
- If possible, let an adult know that you're in the house alone. Unless the phone is out, you should call your parent right away.

### Lights Out!

What to do if the electricity goes off? To get the exciting conclusion to this story you'll have to read the section on BLACK-OUTS. Don't wait! Read it *now!*

◆ NOTES:

*Just*

# Telephone

See PHONE CALLS.

# Theft

See BICYCLES, PUBLIC TRANSPORTATION, and SAFETY AND SECURITY.

# TOASTERS

Everyone knows how to use a toaster. So why talk about it? Only because something goes wrong every once in a while and you should know how to handle it.

## Jam Up

If the bread jams in the toaster, NEVER try to get it out by sticking in a fork or knife, or anything else. You could get a bad electrical shock this way. Not only that, you could damage the toaster, giving your parent a shock. Instead, disconnect the toaster by removing the plug from the outlet. Then get the bread out by gently turning the toaster upside down. (Easy does it: there are a lot of crumbs in there.)

The same is true if the bread starts to smoke, burn, or even catch fire. Discon-

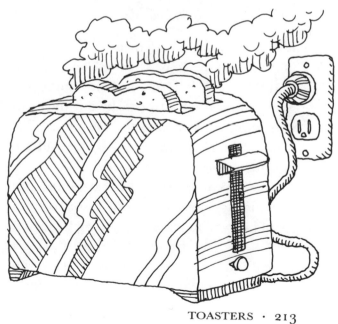

nect the toaster — right away. Then put out the fire with a little water or a fire extinguisher, or smother the fire with a heavy towel.

## Cheese It on the Cheeseburgers

Use your toaster or toaster oven *only* for the things it was meant to do. If your toaster only makes regular old dry toast, don't put in buttered bread. (And forget the jelly!) Never try to squeeze in rolls or odd-shaped pieces of bread: they'll just break up and burn. And if you have a toaster oven, ask your parent what you can — and cannot — make in it. Most toaster ovens are fine for grilled-cheese sandwiches, but were not meant for broiling cheeseburgers!

See also APPLIANCES.

◆ NOTES:

_____
_____
_____
_____
_____

# ～ TOOTH KNOCKED OUT ～

## Save That Tooth!

If you have an accident and one of your permanent teeth is knocked out, try to find the tooth before you leave the scene. Sometimes, the tooth can be put back! In your mouth! Attached to your gums! But it has to be the *whole tooth* — root and all. Not just a piece of the tooth.

You have to keep the knocked-out tooth in a moist piece of cloth or tissue, or in a jar of lukewarm water (anything to keep it wet) until you get it to a dentist. Don't wipe it off. And don't wait. Rush it — and yourself — to your dentist or the emergency room of a hospital. If you get it there within thirty minutes, you have the best chance of saving that tooth.

See also FIRST AID.

# ⌐ TOOTHACHES ⌐

## Oh, My Aching Tooth

When you get a toothache, it's best to tell a parent about it right away. Then your parent will probably call your dentist to make an appointment. Be sure to tell

someone at the dentist's office if the pain is really bad so that the dentist will see you as soon as he/she can. Meanwhile, you can lessen the pain by sucking on some ice. You can also take aspirin — with your parent's permission.

## If I Ignore It, Will It Go Away?

Well, the pain might. But the decay won't. In fact, it may be getting worse and worse, even if you can't feel a thing. So, it's best not to put it off, and to see a dentist right away.

◆ NOTES:

_____
_____
_____
_____
_____
_____

# Trains

See PUBLIC TRANSPORTATION.

*Through*

# ᕙ VACUUM CLEANERS ᕙ

Using a vacuum cleaner is like using a toaster: it's so easy that you *think* you know everything there is to know, even if you don't. You've learned how to turn it on and off (no big deal, unless you're in a hurry and can't find the switch!), how the bag that collects the dirt is changed, and what attachments and settings are used for what jobs. Of course, these instructions will be different for different machines. But here are a few pointers you should also know, for any vaccum cleaner:

• Before using the machine, check the bag inside. If it's full of dirt, empty it or change it.

• Don't vacuum broken glass, china, or anything with sharp edges, which could really mess up the machine. The same goes for small things, like paper clips. With small, *valuable* objects, such as jewelry or coins, there's a double problem: they can hurt the machine *and* the machine can hurt them.

• Never use a vacuum cleaner on a wet floor or try to vacuum up spilled liquids. You could damage the machine and/or get an electrical shock.

See also APPLIANCES.

◆ NOTES:

# Washing Machines

See LAUNDRY.

## ᖇ WORKING PARENTS ᖇ

### Working with Working Parents

If your parents (or parent) work at jobs away from home, they're not always around when you want or need them. They may be working because they need the money, or they may have careers that are very important to them because they allow them to express themselves creatively or to contribute something to the community. Or they may simply prefer working outside the home because they find it interesting.

Whatever the reason, they probably feel bad that they don't have more time for you. You can make it easier on everyone by accepting the situation and by helping to make it work. Here are a few ideas:

• Unless you have a full-time housekeeper, pitch in and help. You could do some of the shopping, cleaning, straightening up — even preparing some of the meals. If you don't have time for any of this, you can still help by getting your schoolwork done without having to be reminded of it.

• Avoid phoning your folks when they're at work. Exceptions: when you're asked to,

and when there's an emergency (call *immediately*). At other times, phone calls merely interfere with their work, disrupt the office or shop, and tie up phone lines.

• If your parents work in the neighborhood, don't just "drop in" on them. Ask first if it's all right, and try not to do it too often.

• Try not to jump all over your parents with problems and complaints the minute they get home. They've just finished a day's work and would probably like to relax for a while. Talk things over with them, but first give them a chance to catch their breath.

• Just as your parents ask you about your day at school, ask them about their day at work: what they do at their jobs, how they like it, whom they work with, and so on. Talking about each other's experiences is a way of sharing and making the time you have together more pleasant.

### Parents Who Work at Home

If one or both of your parents work at home, it's very tempting to interrupt

them, but try not to. Remind yourself that they're doing a job and have to get it done. Don't keep running in with questions like, "Should I have milk or orange juice?" unless your parent doesn't mind constant interruptions. Most do, unless it's really important. Also, try to keep noise (TV, radio, stereo, friends!) down when your parent(s) is working.

If your mother or father stays home to take care of the family and the house, that's a job, too. It involves many skills: cooking, plumbing, repairs, budgeting, and more. Show your mother or father the same consideration you'd show anyone who's working.

*Special Note:* Almost everything in this book is for kids whose parents work: that's one of the reasons it was written. But you might want to pay special attention to the section on EMERGENCIES (to find out when you should — and shouldn't — interrupt) and the section on CHORES (to find out how to help out).

◗ NOTES:

_____
_____
_____
_____
_____

If you're on your own a lot, you may find that you worry about things, and there's often no one to discuss them with. That's not unusual, but it's too bad. Because worrying is a complete waste of time. It doesn't make the problem go away, it doesn't make it get better, and it can make it seem worse than it is.

The next time you hear yourself saying, "I'm worried about . . ." STOP. Ask yourself if there's anything you can do about it.

- If you're worried about flunking math, try studying or getting extra help.
- If you're worried that you might oversleep and miss the school trip, set an alarm clock or ask someone to wake you up (or both).
- If you're worried that your folks won't be able to get you that bike you want so badly, try to find a part-time job and save up the money yourself.

The time you spend worrying gets you nowhere. Doing something usually helps.

### One More Thing

Try not to spend time worrying about what other people think of you. This gets our

No matter how hard you try, you'll never please all the people all the time, and you could end up pleasing no one — including yourself. Earn your own respect by honestly facing your problems, and by making the best decisions you can. In the end, your own opinion of yourself is what really counts.

## Zits

See ACNE.

# ✌ IMPORTANT TELEPHONE NUMBERS ✌

*Fill in whatever is applicable in your area. To make
an emergency phone call, see instructions on page 181.*

☞ PARENT(S): Number(s) where parent(s) can be reached away from home.

_____

_____

_____

☞ ALTERNATES: Numbers of friends, relatives, neighbors when parent(s)
cannot be reached.

_____    _____

_____    _____

_____    _____

☞ FIRE DEPT. _____    _____
☞ POLICE DEPT. _____    _____
☞ POISON CONTROL CENTER _____    _____
☞ HOSPITAL _____    _____
☞ AMBULANCE _____    _____
☞ DOCTOR _____    _____
☞ GAS CO. _____    _____
☞ TELEPHONE CO.: *Emergency* _____    *Other* _____
☞ DRUGSTORE _____    _____
☞ TAXI SERVICE _____    _____
☞ OTHER IMPORTANT PHONE NUMBERS:

_____    _____

_____    _____

_____    _____

_____    _____

## To Kids and Parents

If you have a faster or easier or better way to do something covered in this book, or if you think there's a subject we should have included, but didn't, we'd really like to hear from you. Write us with your suggestions:

Elaine Chaback and Pat Fortunato
c/o Little, Brown and Company
34 Beacon Street
Boston, Massachusetts 02106